Hornbook*
Ethics

D0781028

Hornbook Ethics

Charles E. Cardwell

Hackett Publishing Company, Inc.
Indianapolis/Cambridge

Copyright © 2015 by Hackett Publishing Company, Inc.

18 17 16 15   1 2 3 4 5 6 7

For further information, please address
Hackett Publishing Company, Inc.
P.O. Box 44937
Indianapolis, Indiana 46244-0937

www.hackettpublishing.com

Cover design by Brian Rak
Interior design by Elizabeth L. Wilson
Composition by Aptara, Inc.

Library of Congress Cataloging-in-Publication Data

Cardwell, Charles E.
  Hornbook ethics / Charles E. Cardwell.
     pages cm
  Includes bibliographical references and index.
  ISBN 978-1-62466-372-7 (pbk.) — ISBN 978-1-62466-373-4 (cloth)
  1. Ethics—Textbooks.   I. Title.
  BJ1025.C45 2015
  170—dc23   2014040657

The paper used in this publication meets the minimum requirements of
American National Standard for Information Sciences—Permanence of
Paper for Printed Library Materials, ANSI Z39.48–1984.

♾

Contents

Contents   vii

A Note to Instructors

Contemporary problems provide an engaging entryway into the study of ethics. Today's students need no convincing about the relevance in their lives of topics like abortion, cloning, euthanasia, sexuality, pornography, invidious discrimination, affirmative action, economic justice, capital punishment, the environment, and so on. They likely come to the first day of class already holding strong opinions on some or all of these matters.

And there's the rub. The very idea of a college course covering ethics strikes a number of students as almost absurd. For some, ethics is something arbitrarily imposed by society (and if it is to be studied at all, it should be in a sociology class). For others, ethics comes directly from the Word of God (and they have already picked up in church all they need to know). Most think of ethics as no more than a matter of personal feeling or opinion to which everyone is entitled—no justification necessary or possible.

Given this mindset, immediate exposure to opposing arguments concerning contemporary issues may do no more than reinforce a student's prejudices. It surely does not automatically foster skills of critical analysis and evaluation. To obtain those, we must carefully draw students' attention to any preconceptions and prejudices that clearly hold them back. We must also instruct them in the rudiments of ethics and in the practical reasoning skills necessary to "do" philosophy. And we must do this *before* we can effectively deal with specific problems.

One day, while I was reading a Supreme Court decision, the term "hornbook law" caught my eye. The term alludes to secondary sources intended for law students. These sources cover basic legal principles and the development of law, but not cutting-edge issues. They do not provide the sort of scholarship that might be found in a law journal, but they do cover more than might be found in a legal encyclopedia. The term "hornbook" originally referred to a child's primer made of parchment protected by a transparent plate made of horn. Today, the term generally denotes a primer that provides instruction in the rudiments or basic skills of a branch of knowledge.

It struck me that beginners desperately need a new hornbook for ethics. The need for ethics primers has long existed and has been served more or less well in various ways. But it has recently become more acute, and more difficult to meet, because today's students have grown up in a world where audio and video media overshadow the written word. These "digital natives" have been reared to think visually and intuitively. They expect to be entertained. They are "aliens" when it comes to critical thinking and the linguistic arts. They struggle to read for comprehension, and they find most strange the idea that one might work out ideas through the process of writing and rewriting. Previously available ethics primers simply do not prepare such students to understand, analyze, and evaluate philosophical work. The present work is intended to do so, at least at the most elementary level.

Hornbook Ethics evolved over more than a decade of classroom experimentation. The overriding principles in its development were threefold:

1) The content would be strictly limited to *rudiments* with a focus on *basic skills*.

2) The presentation would be *guided by what works* as determined by feedback from questions students ask in class, the direction of classroom discussion, and the quality of responses to short-answer exams.

3) The exposition should be as brief and unfussy as possible, with chapter length kept to a minimum—even at the expense of dividing closely related discussions over multiple chapters.

Following these principles formed the work in ways that I did not anticipate and brought some unconventional elements into the result. Chapter 1, for example, devotes more than the customary effort to establishing that ethics and scripture are not essentially identical.

Again, one might expect the materials in Chapters 2, 3, and 4 to be condensed and united into a single chapter on logic. However, in keeping with the principles enunciated above, division into three chapters seemed wise. Length aside, the content itself ended up being somewhat unusual. Early versions focused quite conventionally on specific forms of inference and on the usual informal fallacies. Students zoned out! I then experimented with more general discussions about language and the elements of rational persuasion. I emphasized differences between normative and descriptive language, the necessity of finding common starting points, of recognizing that disagreements can arise regarding concepts, facts, principles, and reasoning itself, and

that each of these can and must be approached and resolved in its own way. This approach turned out to be effective in a transformative way, changing students' attitudes towards the possibility of defending and supporting an ethical view—and even in evaluating its merit!

Whenever possible, I have found it effective to let the text serve as its own example. Thus, Chapter 5 itself illustrates the substance of the preceding three chapters as it introduces and analyzes a number of basic normative predicates—is good/bad, is right/wrong, is legal/illegal, is ethical/unethical, is moral/immoral—which are commonly conflated or muddled together. This illustration drives home the point that one can discuss ethics in a productive way.

For me, using the first five chapters as they finally evolved has produced one very important outcome: I no longer need repeatedly revisit issues of feeling and opinion as we go through ten weeks discussing the "hot" topics that comprise the main body of the course.[1]

After basic skills, *Hornbook* turns to rudiments. Aristotle's *Nicomachean Ethics*, the first systematic treatment of ethics, in effect defined the discipline and set the stage for what was to come. *Hornbook*'s Chapter 6 lays out a unifying general approach to ethical theories that comes from Aristotle, an approach that I have not seen used in other introductory texts. Each perspective is approached through a consideration of what it takes to be the highest good and how that good serves as the root from which morality grows. Each perspective is also linked to reasons one might present in its support as well as the most compelling objections to it.

Chapter 6 also introduces virtue ethics and the Golden Mean. Chapter 7 considers the views of relativists and others who reject the idea that a morality-defining good exists. The divine command theory is included here as a special case of individual relativism. Chapter 8 turns to consequentialism (including Mill's utilitarianism). Several cases begin to draw out concrete differences among approaches. Deontology (with emphasis on Kant) is introduced in Chapter 9. Utilitarianism and deontology are presented as works in progress. The unifying approach introduced in Chapter 6 opens the door to a clear and compelling explanation of Kant's two main forms of the

---

1. These discussions flow from assigned articles that defend opposing sides of each topic. Such articles are to be found in any number of excellent anthologies or in online databases (such as JSTOR) available to students through most college libraries. *Hornbook Ethics* serves to prepare students for productive engagement in such discussions.

Categorical Imperative, showing that they really are the same idea as seen from different perspectives. (I believe this is an original and unique element in *Hornbook*.) Rights-based analysis is presented as the flipside of duty-based analysis. Chapter 10 wraps things up with a way to apply ethical theory to real-world cases. It reprises an approach to practical reasoning that was quite popular a few years back: evaluating moral situations by way of four moral principles: autonomy, nonmaleficence, beneficence, and justice. Appendices summarize the critical thinking chapters, expand the treatment of deductive inference, and offer suggestions for further reading.

Hornbook is not intended as a reference book, a history, or a comprehensive account of ethics. It is simply and unapologetically a primer: designed for novices and intended to prepare them to analyze and evaluate real-life ethical problems. I developed the text by using it not only with general education students in freshmen ethics, but also with nursing students in biomedical ethics and business students in business ethics.

Throughout the text, I have maintained a lighthearted tone and, in accord with the concept of a hornbook, have consciously avoided the sort of sophistication and subtlety that would reinforce the novice's idea that philosophy boils down to nitpicking. The content and organization are as they are as a result of extensive classroom experimentation and development.

Undoubtedly, the greatest challenge in developing *Hornbook* has been to avoid misleading readers through the omissions and simplifications that the hornbook concept requires. I have done my best to eliminate as much potential for misunderstanding as possible. I also recognize that whatever can be misunderstood will be misunderstood. This corollary of Murphy's Law virtually guarantees that misunderstandings will still occur. When they do, I would like to make repairs. Please write me at cecardwell@pstcc.edu to report any problems or offer suggestions for improvement.

Acknowledgments

Through class discussion and test responses, hundreds of students over the last decade or so revealed what was working and, more importantly, what was not working in earlier drafts of *Hornbook*. I am grateful for their unknowing participation in forging the work into its present form. I am also grateful for contributions from Heidi Speck and Peter Tramel; each passed along extensive notes that revealed infelicities and sources of potential misinterpretation or confusion in the penultimate draft. Frank Mashburn and I talked for hours about the relationships between religion and ethics, and these discussions heavily influenced my treatment of the topic. I also gained useful insights as a consequence of discussions with David Howell, Court Lewis, and Adam Turk. Brian Rak, Editorial Director at Hackett, suggested many improvements in both clarity and content. Whenever needed, Heather Schroeder helped me find the right words to match my thoughts. Cathy Cardwell found dozens of typos and other errors long after I was certain that all had been eliminated. Finally, Liz Wilson and Harbour Fraser Hodder eliminated the innumerable stylistic inconsistencies that I threw at them and so added a valuable aesthetic dimension to the work. Thanks to all these folks, *Hornbook* is much better than it otherwise would have been.

1. WHAT IS ETHICS?

I   The Central Question

Much human activity starts with problems. Problems related to ownership and exchange of land and goods, for example, might lead to activities such as developing land surveys, creating markets, inventing basic accounting, and establishing dispute-resolving courts. Specific problems may inspire wildly different "solutions." Consider death. Religion and medicine tackle Death from opposite sides: one seeks to find meaning in the face of death; the other struggles to prevent, or at least postpone, the inevitable as much as possible. Further, a variety of distinct problems might be attacked through a single activity; thus, magic—a primordial problem-solving tool—has been invoked for a host of problems, from manipulating the physical environment, to curing disease, to influencing the gods. Eventually, humans begin to wonder why some attempted solutions work but others do not. This sort of wonder underlies theoretical disciplines such as those that we find in academia, including (to continue the ownership and exchange example) geometry, arithmetic, management theory, economics, and jurisprudence.

Roughly two and a half millennia ago in Greece, the philosophical discipline that we now call ETHICS grew out of a new approach to a very old problem: **How does one live a good life?** Answering this central question would tell us how we *ought* to live...and that would be, in Socrates words, "no small matter."

To pose the question is easy; to answer it is not. Ultimately, any answer demands that we figure out what it is to be fully human, and that raises a myriad of ancillary questions: How do humans differ from other beings? Do we govern ourselves by reason, or do instinct and emotion rule? What do we value? What role do social institutions play in shaping our being? And so on.

These ancillary questions are, to a degree, answerable through experience, observation, or experiment—that is, they are *empirical* questions. Historians, anthropologists, psychologists, sociologists, and political scientists all study them. The social sciences provide much useful information as to what is possible. They reveal the scope of human behavior across the world and throughout the ages. But empirical science, properly speaking, is limited to description. **Descriptive claims** present a picture, account, or report. They depend upon the methodologies of empirical observation for justification.

Except for the funnies and the op-ed pages, newspapers are supposed to limit themselves to description: The legislature failed to pass a budget bill. The FDA has approved a new medication. Three persons died when a semi-truck collided head-on with a compact car. The home team beat the visitors.... Schools also concentrate on description: George Washington was the first President of the United States. A body continues in its state of rest or motion unless acted upon by an outside force. The temperature of the egg during incubation determines the sex of a newborn alligator.... In the sense of the old adage, "Judge not, lest ye be judged," descriptive claims make no judgments. They are, as we say, "value neutral."

Descriptions have their limits. A description may tell us how to reach a goal; it cannot tell us what goals to seek. It can tell us what people have done; it cannot tell us unconditionally what people *should* or *should not* do, or *whether* or *why* they should or should not do it. Empirical science can tell us something of what people have become. It can identify historical events that have influenced behaviors and suggest how these events may have done so. But science cannot tell us what people should strive to become—or why. It cannot answer questions such as "What should we value?" or "What justifies our social institutions?" These are normative matters. **Normative claims** prescribe or imply some criteria (or criterion) by which something can be ranked, valued, or judged. The central question of ethics asks what makes a good life. This question demands a normative response. Normative issues reach beyond the scientific purview.

Because the normative goes beyond the scientific, one must look beyond empirical methods to justify normative claims. And because the descriptive and the normative require different sorts of justifications, it is important to notice which is which. Remember, normative expressions prescribe or imply rank, value, or judgment; descriptive claims present a value-neutral picture, account, or report.[1]

Terms like "good" and "evil" are by nature normative...they always express a judgment. "Kill" is descriptive, but "murder" is normative. To say that Peyton Manning quarterbacked the 2007 Super Bowl Champions is to be descriptive; to say that Manning is the best quarterback in the history of football is to be normative. Some expressions may be used either descriptively or normatively; one must look at the meaning, not just the words, to decide the matter. When my neighbor tells me his bulldog is a "champion[2] bitch," he is being descriptive; but if he calls his wife a "champion bitch," he absolutely issues a normative judgment.

It should be noted that philosophical ethics is not the only normative discipline. Normative claims crop up widely in human discourse, perhaps most obviously in literary, film, art, and music criticism, in law, in politics, and in religion. Normative claims are also common in accounting, finance, marketing, business management, political economics, and a host of other human enterprises. The exchange of goods in markets, for example, turns completely on comparisons of value. Indeed, normative claims play an essential role in all disciplines. Thus, in the sciences, the very demand for objectivity is a normative demand. Moreover, purely normative considerations lead scientists to accept or reject specific empirical methodologies in specific cases. (Must we design a "double blind" experiment here?) And finally, after publication, scientific research studies are normatively praised as "good" or normatively condemned as "flawed."

Clearly, the normative plays a central role in our lives but often lies "under the radar" and gets little direct attention. This is stunning, considering that normative elements underlie all human activity. Values, after all, furnish the sole motivation for action. If we valued nothing, we would

---

1. Do not confuse distinctions between the descriptive and the normative with alleged distinctions between fact and opinion. Both the descriptive—e.g., "Life exists outside of our solar system"—and the normative—e.g., "Life is beautiful"—may (sometimes) be subjects of opinion; it is also quite possible that, in addition to certain descriptive claims, certain normative claims—e.g., "Murder is morally wrong"—may be matters of fact. Since the descriptive need not be factual and the normative need not be opinion (or vice versa), the distinctions are fundamentally different.

2. We assume for this illustration that the dog has been (normatively) judged "best" in an officially sanctioned dog show. Once the dog has won the honor, the previously normative term becomes descriptive.

do nothing…not even eat. Without the normative, we would be dead. That's significant. Ethical claims are inherently normative and we shall soon consider how they may, in general, be justified. Before doing so, however, let us look at traditional reservoirs of advice about a good life.

II   Art and Religion

Every culture, forged over generations by the collective experiences of a people, captures its insights in the arts and in the religious beliefs and practices that shape each succeeding generation. The culture into which a person is born informs his or her core intuitions as to what makes a good life. Ancient man transmitted folk wisdom through myths, legends, and religion. Today, the arts—music, dance, storytelling, poetry, photography, sculpture, painting—and religion still serve this role. Art and religion can be both powerful and engaging: they can enrich our imaginations, suggest possibilities, and perhaps motivate us to action. The arts drive us emotionally towards (or away from) a particular understanding of life with appealing (or repulsing) portrayals of life's possibilities. One who seeks deeper *justification* for a particular belief or behavior, however, will find frustration in the arts: they typically make no attempt to explain *why* we should—or even *if* we should—take these portrayals as models for our lives.

What about religion? The scope and variety of religious belief and practice covers an almost incomprehensible range. As to the existence of spirits or gods, for example, beliefs range all the way from animism (which accepts the existence of countless spirits inhabiting innumerable objects and beings) to atheism (which accepts the existence of none). The scope and variety in use of the term "religion" can be equally baffling. To make some sense of it, imagine a tree grown of beliefs and practices. Each branch of the tree shares the beliefs and practices of the branch from which it grows, but each branch also differentiates itself by adding new beliefs and practices. From the trunk, main branches form with core beliefs of "world religions" (Christianity, Islam, Hinduism, and Buddhism, among others).[3]

---

3. Primary branches might also be formed with generic belief categories (such as monotheism, henotheism, theological dualism, polytheism, deism, etc.) common in religious taxonomies.

From these primary branches, additional beliefs and practices gener-
ate secondary branches. Thus, Buddhism branches into the Thera-
vada, Mahayana, and Vajrayana traditions; Christianity branches into
Roman Catholicism, Eastern Orthodoxy, and Protestantism; and so
on. Branching can stop at any point, but it also may continue. Tertiary
branching gives us, for example, the belief sets of Methodist, Presby-
terian, Baptist, and other Protestant Christian denominations. Any
given branch may (or may not) have associated with it an institution
that supports, interprets, and perhaps proselytizes the specific set of
beliefs and practices forming that branch.

In its most general sense, the term "religion" references this tree,
taken abstractly and in its entirety, together with all institutions and
experiences associated with it. More narrowly, the collective beliefs
and practices that make up any given branch of this tree may be called
"a religion" as may any institution[4] that supports, interprets, and perhaps proselytizes a specific set of beliefs and practices. Almost anything associated with the tree may be called "religious," including
profoundly personal spiritual or mystical experiences not necessarily
associated with a particular institution or set of beliefs.

Clearly, this sort of tree model could also be used for science or
philosophy or any number of areas unrelated to religion. What then
distinguishes the "religion" tree from the "science" or other trees?[5]
The answer lies in what the tree grows from. Religion is rooted in the
frightening certainty that each of us will eventually die.[6] The world's
great wealth of religious belief and practice reflects the vast range of
possibilities that give meaning and understanding to this certainty. As
it turns out, there are many ways to find meaning and understanding in death without addressing the matter of how to live a good life,
and many religions pay little if any attention to this matter. However,
among religions that find death to be a gateway to another life (perhaps

---

4. Or even an informal collection of individuals.

5. Many scholars seek to understand religion genetically by studying its divine, its
psychological, and/or its primitive anthropological origins. Others approach religion
by studying the way it actually functions in addressing human needs (see William H.
Bernhardt's *Functional Philosophy of Religion*, Criterion Press, 1958). This functional
approach underlies the present discussion.

6. More precisely, religion is rooted in the horrendous, nonmanipulable elements of
human existence, the most universal of which is death. William Calloley Tremmel's
seminal book, *Religion: What Is It?* (first edition, Holt, Rinehart and Winston, 1976)
presents a compelling argument for this view.

in eternity, perhaps in reincarnation in this world), and which believe that the quality of this life determines the quality of the next, the question of how to live a good life can become one of central importance.

So, how does one live a good life? In religion we find a plethora of often conflicting answers.[7] In the vast majority of cases, the source urges us to accept its answer because of its authority in such matters. Appeal to authority is (as we shall see) always problematic; it is especially so in cases of conflict. What do you do when your mother tells you to do one thing and your father tells you to do the opposite? How do you decide? Which authority do you accept as authentic? Both parents claim authentic authority, so you cannot use that; rather, you must find some independent basis of choice. The same holds when religious authorities are in conflict.

Even when where is no immediate issue regarding conflict, appeal to authority can be problematic.[8] Lt. William Calley, charged with committing war crimes in what has come to be called the My Lai[9] Massacre, defended his actions by appeal to authority in the person of his commanding officer. Calley claimed that he simply followed orders to clear the village. The prosecution contended that Calley should have seen that these orders, if they were in fact as he understood them to be, would be inauthentic[10] under the higher authority of military law, and so they should have been disobeyed (as military law demands). The fact is that authorities can be mistaken and so issue inauthentic information or commands. When that happens, authentication cannot come from the authority.

Other problems arise if inaccuracies can creep in when information is copied or translated before being passed along. Here again, appeal to authority breaks down; one must look beyond the authority to verify accuracy. Furthermore, especially when authority resides in a document, issues of scope and meaning may come to the fore. The U.S. Supreme Court constantly struggles with both of these as the justices deal with cases involving situations that the founding fathers could

---

7. Conflicting answers are by no means limited to religion; religion is here mentioned simply as the subject presently being considered.

8. *Authority* is a complex notion that invites ambiguity, both between power and expertise and between power or expertise and its possessor. These ambiguities each raise difficulties with respect to any appeal to authority.

9. A village in Viet Nam.

10. Indeed, in this case, illegal.

never have imagined. Does a passage in the Constitution include within its scope the matter before the Court? What exactly does this or that word or passage mean? Similar problems arise in understanding scripture, especially regarding passages that employ allegory, metaphor, simile, or other literary devices. Issues of meaning may have been at the core of the Calley case. Perhaps he simply misunderstood the proper import of "to clear a village."

In sum, issues of **authenticity**, **accuracy**, **scope**, and **meaning** introduce uncertainty about anything supported by appeal to authority, including religious teachings. Religion is far from oblivious to the problems just outlined: Theologians struggle with them every day. If we are to discover what makes a good life, must we struggle with them too?

That depends. Ultimately, religions depend on **faith**.[11] They may uplift, admonish, and/or inspire, but they do not persuade us by reason.[12] If we turn to religious authority for answers, we find disagreement and even contradiction. Thus, if we must depend upon religious authority for our answer to what makes a good life, and if we have no reason to accept an answer other than that some religious (or other) authority has given it, we are trapped in an impasse. But if a good life would be a good life even if no religious authority had ever thought or spoken about the matter, then the foundation for a good life would be independent of religion, and we should be able to find its elements by use of our own wit and reason. This is exactly what ETHICS, as a philosophical discipline, seeks to do.

11. In "The Will to Believe" (1896), William James compares beliefs deriving from our passional character with those deriving from our intellect. Beliefs of the intellect are a product of reason and experience. We cannot modify them by will. Passional beliefs, by contrast, are non-rational. "The heart has its reasons of which reason knows nothing" wrote Pascal. Faith, as we understand it here, is what is perceived by the heart rather than by reason. Put another way, faith is that faculty of mind whereby we gain beliefs that reason cannot deliver.

12. Tertullian's *Credo quia absurdum* ("I believe because it is absurd") exemplifies the fact that the use of reason is not essential to religion. Nevertheless, many religions aspire to provide a foundation based upon reason, or at least to show that their beliefs are not contrary to reason. Wide use of the Wesleyan Quadrilateral (scripture, tradition, reason, and experience) as an aid to understanding specific religions (especially from a believer's perspective) recognizes reason as a common element of religious belief. (Tertullian (c. 160–c. 225), an early Christian apologist, is often regarded as the father of Latin Christianity. John Wesley (1703–1791), an Anglican theologian, founded the evangelical movement known as Methodism.)

III   The Founders

In the Greek culture that had grown up around the Aegean Sea about two and a half millennia ago, **Socrates** (c. 470–399 B.C.E.) began to look at living a good life in a new way. Rather than make pronouncements regarding rules of behavior, he struggled to discover the essential nature of things such as virtue and vice, right and wrong, justice and injustice, good and evil, and problems like whether it is possible to teach people how to live well.

Socrates and his peers and successors who took on these problems, effectively invented the discipline that we in the West call ETHICS. Socrates' student, **Plato** (429–347 B.C.E), developed the Socratic approach in literary dialogues,[13] which discuss the matters mentioned just above. Plato's student, **Aristotle** (384–322 B.C.E.),[14] seems to have been the first to lay out the whole subject in a systematic way. His *Nicomachean Ethics* sets the stage upon which all subsequent writers on ethics play. (We shall return to Aristotle shortly.)

IV   Terminology

What then is ETHICS?[15] For a first approximation, consider endeavors to study matters related to the question of how to live a good life. These endeavors can be divided into two broad categories[16] with quite different methodology and objectives: Descriptive ethics concerns

---

13. The Platonic dialogues most relevant to ETHICS are: *Crito, Euthyphro, Gorgias, Meno, Protagoras,* and *The Republic.*

14. Plato and Aristotle often found significantly different solutions to the same problems.

15. To my knowledge, there is no simple, fully accepted definition of the term "ethics." Dictionaries give a number of meanings that range across (at least) beliefs, codes, rules, motives, and conduct, as these may be related to either individuals or groups; the term also applies to the systematic study of these. To avoid confusion, it pays to be context-aware.

16. The following is one of a number of possible taxonomies for disciplines called "ethics"; none are universally accepted.

matters that fall within the scientific purview. Philosophical ethics covers matters that go beyond science. More specifically:

Descriptive ethics categorizes and describes actual behaviors and beliefs. It makes no value judgments; it may tell us what some people value, but says nothing about whether the values are worthy or not. In short, descriptive ethics tells only what is the case; it does not offer *shoulds* or *oughts*.[17] Anthropologists, psychologists, economists, and sociologists do descriptive ethics when they report on the mores, practices, and beliefs of individuals or societies.

Philosophical ethics[18] also splits rather naturally into two categories: normative ethics and ethical theory or metaethics.

Normative ethics (in contrast to descriptive ethics) focuses on *shoulds* and *oughts*, values and judgments, "thou shalts" and "thou shalt nots." It dissects concrete cases and tries to discover what actions should or should not be done, are or are not morally acceptable, required, or prohibited; it assesses dispositions, actions, ends, objects, and states of affairs; it advocates particular foundational principles, moral codes, and rules; and it engages in *casuistry*, the evaluation of acts through subsumption under such rules. Normative ethics is evidently a very old enterprise, tracing far back into preliterate times.

Ethical theory (metaethics) also deals extensively with normative issues, but it has a different focus than normative ethics. Ethical theory examines the degree to which normative ethics is possible and, when appropriate, provides support to the normative undertaking. It probes the legitimacy of various modes of reasoning; it works toward clear and precise definition of terms; it examines the meaning of ethical claims—their truth or falsity, their objectivity or subjectivity; it investigates the possibility of finding common ethical standards and systematizing these under first principles; and it applies theories to analyze practical cases.[19] It was, for all intents and purposes, invented

---

17. Thus, descriptive ethics does not itself make ethical claims; rather it reports on claims of an ethical nature that it finds in its target population.

18. It would seem natural to contrast "descriptive ethics" with "normative ethics," especially since what we are calling "philosophical ethics" is a normative discipline. We do not do so because the name "normative ethics" has been taken by longstanding use for the subcategory so labeled in what follows.

19. This last activity is sometimes called **applied ethics** and may be listed in other taxonomies as a third category under philosophical ethics.

by Socrates and his peers. When we use ETHICS without a qualifier, we (usually) refer to this discipline. Thus, in this book, *Hornbook Ethics*, the use of the term ETHICS denotes what we have just called ethical theory or metaethics (including applied ethics).

Life would go on without these divisions, but not as well. They are worthwhile because they highlight important differences among concepts, facts, and values. In so doing, they help us understand under which circumstances each of these may be called for as we probe into ethical issues.

2. WIT

How can one live a good life? The arts, religion, and "society" offer answers, but lack *whys* or lack unquestionable authenticity. If we are to find a compelling answer, therefore, we must turn to our natural ability to perceive and understand—that is, to our wit—and to our reason. Before we attempt our own answer to the central question, it will pay us to examine the power and limitations of wit and reason.

I Truth

In making a claim, whether descriptive or normative, one presents that claim as a truth. The truth of a claim is a function of what's what in reality. When I assert, for example, "water is two parts hydrogen and one part oxygen," the truth of my claim depends upon whether water really is made up of hydrogen and oxygen in the ratio of two to one. That is, if what I say corresponds to reality, I have spoken a truth; if not, I have spoken a falsehood.

Discovering truth turns out to be a very troublesome task. None of us has a direct pipeline to reality. We depend upon sense and reason...and both sense and reason can mislead us. Mirages and illusions teach that seeing something with your own eyes isn't necessarily seeing what really is the case. There is, however, a *practical standard* for accepting a claim as true: universal agreement among serious, unprejudiced investigators. Universality is crucial. One individual may undertake a serious investigation and nevertheless produce mistaken results. But when a number of serious, independent investigators agree on the outcome, we properly conclude that individual errors have been eliminated and the claim (almost surely) does correspond to reality.

II   Common Ground

How do serious investigators come to agree? Well, for one thing, they undertake *serious* investigation. But even before serious investigation is possible, investigators must establish common ground. Shared experience common to all parties underlies scientific objectivity. To understand red and green, one must recognize red and green and some of their relationships with other recognizable entities. One cannot tell a blind man enough about red or green so that he can fully comprehend the notions. That is, one cannot define these terms; rather, they serve as a common starting point for inquiry. Without such common starting points, understood without definition, there could be no definitions, and more importantly, there could be no meeting of minds…hence no agreement…hence no practical standard of truth.

The "hard" sciences—physics, chemistry, mathematics, and so on—all depend upon practitioners beginning with a common set of undefined terms that are (or at least are thought to be) understood and recognized by all. In physics, these are terms like "mass" and "force" and "charge" … in geometry, "point" and "line" and "plane." We must agree what all of these terms mean—that is, what they pick out or point to in the world—if we are to communicate and if we are to find truth.

The need for common ground underlies all serious inquiry. Science is often presented as a cold body of indisputable fact. But the growth of science has been slow and fraught with controversy. Controversy is resolved by discovering common ground and working from there. The same is true of all disciplines and all successful attempts at conflict resolution. That is, the need to work from common ground applies as much to the normative as to the descriptive. In this way, the two are perhaps not as different as one might first think. All human knowledge, whether descriptive or normative, must ultimately be grounded in our common wit, reason, and experience.

III   Positions

As we have seen, ethical claims are inherently normative. We have also seen that **normative claims** play an important role in many areas of our lives, and that the methodologies of empirical science, which (when properly applied) so beautifully justify descriptive claims about our world, fall short in the normative domain. In addition, we have seen that justification requires working from common ground. How then might we go about justifying normative claims?

A sometimes popular view holds that normative claims cannot be justified. The reason, it is said, is that normative claims express nothing more than naked, subjective **opinion**. It may further be claimed that opinion is just opinion and cannot be justified. Fortunately for us (since normative elements underlie essentially all human activity), this view is mistaken. A normative claim may at first look like a mere opinion; nevertheless, it need not be naked and purely subjective. If one can discover some intersubjectively agreed to (i.e., objective) common ground and apply critical analysis and cogent reasoning, the claim becomes (so to speak) fully clothed, and may properly be called a **position**. Positions, though superficially opinion-like, differ from mere opinions in clarity, precision, and justification.

Conceptual analysis brings clarity and precision to a position. Reasons and reasoning bring justification. Reasons may come as facts or as principles. Hence, to establish a position, common ground must be found in four realms: concepts, facts, principles, and reasoning. Let's consider each of these.

IV   Concepts

Before one can reasonably begin to justify a claim (whether descriptive or normative), one must determine what the claim amounts to. That is, one must use critical analysis to "get clear" on relevant concepts.

Concepts comprise the very stuff of our thoughts and the basis for our actions. Mistaken or inappropriate concepts can lead to disaster. Aviator Wolfgang Langeweische (1907–2002) devotes nearly 380 pages in his classic *Stick and Rudder* (1944) to correcting the mistaken idea that the elevator controls an airplane's altitude (in fact, it sets the in-flight airspeed) and that the throttle controls speed (actually, it affects altitude). Langeweische blames most fatal aircraft accidents on pilots' confused concepts as to these control functions.

Not limited merely to matters of life and death, conceptual questions often have more broadly fundamental significance as well. Albert Einstein's famous 1905 paper,[1] which presented the theory of special relativity and revolutionized physics, begins with a basic conceptual question: "What is simultaneity?" The analysis of this concept provided the basis from which the whole theory of relativity was derived. As with relativity, the greatest advances in scientific theory have often resulted directly from a successful attack on some conceptual question.

V Questions

A **question** may be a point in dispute, an issue, a doubt, a problem, a concern, or an entity used to bring one of these to attention. In any case, wrong or unimportant questions beget wrong or unimportant answers; perspicuous questions open doors to progress. Wisdom demands keen understanding of questions. Understanding requires distinguishing various types of questions and considering appropriate procedures for answering each type.

Linguistic form may not necessarily be a reliable guide as to what a question is really about. Note the parallels in the following:

> Case A. Lee, engaged to be married but thinking the engagement to be a happy secret, is congratulated by a friend: "How do you know Pat and I are engaged?" Lee asks. "Pat told me," the friend replies.

> Case B. Lee, having suffered a sequence of tragedies and doubting God's existence, seeks council from a minister: "How do you know God loves me?" Lee asks. "God told me," the minister replies.

In Case A, the reply seems quite satisfactory. There is no doubt about Pat's existence and the fact of engagement. What is wanted is a biographical account of how that particular person became aware of the

---

1. Einstein, Albert (1905). "Zur Elektrodynamik bewegter Körper." *Annalen der Physik* 17 (10): 891–921.

facts. By contrast, the reply in Case B is unsatisfactory. It is unsatisfactory just because it misconstrues the kind of question that is being asked. Here, biographical data is irrelevant. It is the very truth of the proposition under consideration that is in question. Evidence directly available only to a selected few will not convince. Only evidence potentially available to anyone willing to take the trouble to obtain it will do.

As these cases suggest, a good way to begin understanding questions is to consider what could answer them. Suppose I am thinking of hiring you to work for my moving company. "Can you lift any given piece of furniture in this room?" I ask. We find out by having you try to lift each piece of furniture. If you lift them all, the answer is "yes." If you try but fail to lift one or more pieces, the answer is "no." Questions that can in principle be answered simply by looking, trying, measuring, or by some such empirical procedure are properly called **empirical** (or often, somewhat misleadingly, factual) **questions**. Note the "in principle": empirical questions may not be answerable in practice. If I ask how many persons will be within the boundaries of Washington, D.C., at high noon on July Fourth next year, though there is in principle a way to find out this information (wait until noon on the Fourth and count 'em), in practice, the best we can do is estimate.

VI   Facts

On the face of it, empirical questions seem pretty straightforward. As it turns out, however, they are only straightforward when the underlying concepts are clear and precise. Sometimes an apparently factual question is really a conceptual question.

To illustrate, consider an event like one described by William James:[2] A child saw a squirrel jump onto the far side of a tree trunk. Hoping to get a better look at the rodent, the child began to run in circles around the tree. The wily squirrel, however, clung to the trunk and scurried around it, keeping himself continuously hidden from the child's view.

---

2. This story differs in minor detail from the one William James (1842–1910, a founding father both of American pragmatism and of the science of psychology) presented in his 1904 lecture entitled "What Pragmatism Means."

Clearly, both the child and the squirrel *circled* the tree trunk. But did the child *circle* the squirrel?

This sounds like a straightforward question of empirical fact. But observers of the event began to dispute the answer. They cited various undisputed points as evidence for their views, yet nobody was swayed. The arguments failed because the real problem was conceptual, not factual. Some observers evidently thought of "to circle" as something like "to be successively to the south, west, north, east, and south of." Others implicitly understood "to circle" as meaning something like "to be successively in front of, to the left of, behind, to the right of, and in front of." Under the former concept, the child does circle the squirrel; under the latter, the child does not. Here is a case where *the fact depends in part upon the concept*: once the concept is agreed upon, the fact is no longer subject to dispute.

Facts, then, depend both on concepts and the state of the world. Once the concepts are clear, we can discover the state of the world by ordinary observation—touching, tasting, smelling, hearing, and seeing—and by its more sophisticated versions as developed by the sciences.

VII   Words

We cannot communicate directly with **concepts**; we must use words instead. Misunderstandings arise when the words that one person uses to mention a concept elicit a different concept in the mind of the hearer. Talk connected with God is so often frustrating because there may be much verbal agreement, but little meeting of the minds. If we agree that "God created the world," we may nevertheless not understand each other. I may think that God created the world complete, in one fell swoop, whereas you may think that God created the world by establishing certain natural processes that led by a long and steady process of evolution to life as we know it. Thus, though we agree on the words, we differ as to the concept of creation. Eventually, different concepts lead to disagreement even on words. When that happens, we wonder how the disagreement arose. We thought we agreed on the fundamentals. In fact, we have not agreed on the fundamentals at all.

The pervasiveness of muddled concepts and resulting general confusion may partially account for the opinion that normative claims cannot be justified. The first steps towards justification, therefore, must be to ferret out the relevant concepts, to refine or sharpen each, and to agree on what words we will use for each. Otherwise, we won't know what we are talking about and are likely to say foolish things.

The necessity of using words to discuss concepts calls for some understanding of semantics. **Semantics** is the study of meanings. Semantic disputes are to be carefully distinguished from mere verbal disputes. Semantic disputes are in no way trivial; they concern our analysis and understanding of concepts. Verbal disputes occur when there is no confusion about what's what in reality, only a tiff over what word to use. Only such verbal tiffs deserve the kind of dismissal the phrase "it's only semantics" is often used to make. If the dispute is truly one of semantics, it is likely to be at the very heart of a substantive conceptual problem. (To avoid confusion, it might be wise to avoid the expression "it's just semantics" and use "it's a verbal problem" instead.)

An illustration may help to draw the distinction. People disagree over whether computers can think. Is the disagreement merely verbal, or is it semantical? Of course, you can always trivialize the question by stipulating that your use of "think" includes what computers do. But this begs the real questions. Words change in meaning over time; nevertheless, at any one period, they do have quite standard uses. Communication is possible only because of this fact. If you want to stick to the ordinary meaning of "think," you must find out what concept (or concepts) that word ordinarily picks out. Only then can you begin to decide the matter.

VIII   Connotation, Emotive Import, and Non-Standard Usage

Words both denote and connote. **Denotation** comprises the literal, primary, or core meaning of a word, whereas **connotation** comprises the feelings or figurative ideas that a word evokes. Connotations commonly add inexplicit normative color to a claim. Often this normative element calls up powerful emotions, and these emotions can cloud our

thinking. Sometimes persons choose words more for their connotations than for their denotative meaning. This practice, especially when
it is unrecognized or unacknowledged, can greatly hinder any genuine
effort to answer serious questions regarding how to live a good life.

Consider hyperbole—extravagant exaggeration. When it is clear
that a claim is exaggerated and not to be taken literally (e.g., it took
forever for the page to download), hyperbole seems harmless. But
when it is not clear that exaggeration is present, hyperbole may seri-
ously mislead or misdirect. Some anti-abortionists, for example, emotionally proclaim that abortion is murder. Presumably, nothing more
needs to be said, since murder is both illegal and immoral. But the
plausibility of this claim depends upon muddled concepts hidden in
misused words.

The word "murder" may be bandied about carelessly in ordinary con-
versation, but its core meaning can be found in any good dictionary:[3]
To murder is to kill a person unlawfully, with malice and premeditation. This means that an execution in accord with and following due
process of law is not murder; it is lawful. To kill a coyote that has been
raiding the chicken house may involve malice and premeditation, but
it is not murder; a coyote is not a person. A person killed in an auto-
mobile accident is not murdered; there is neither malice nor premeditation. (Notice that "kill" is a descriptive term whereas "murder" is a
normative one.)

To abort is, in general, to terminate a process before it has run its
full course. Thus, an airplane pilot may abort a landing if a cow wanders onto the landing strip. To abort a pregnancy, then, is to terminate
the pregnancy before it has run its full term. While such termination
usually does result in the death of an embryo or fetus, it need not do
so: in some cases of abortion by hysterotomy, the fetus has survived. If
there is no death, there is no killing and hence there can be no murder.

What if an embryo or fetus is killed as a result of an abortion? Perhaps one could commit murder by abortion just as one could commit
murder by strangulation (for example), but it is by no means obvious
that one could do so. Murder is unlawful, but the vast majority of
abortions are legally performed, so they cannot be murders. Murder
requires malice,[4] but the vast majority of abortions clearly involve no

---

3. See, for example, http://www.merriam-webster.com/dictionary/murder. The legal
definition of *murder* comes directly from the ordinary-language one.

4. Unlawful homicide without malice or premeditation is called *manslaughter*.

malice, so they cannot be murders. And finally, if a zygote, embryo, or fetus is not a person, terminating its life cannot be murder.

Undoubtedly, the "abortion is murder" anti-abortionist would suppose that any human life lost in an abortion is the life of a person. But this notion is widely disputed by those who contend that an early fetus is no more a person than an amoeba, jellyfish, or tadpole is. One cannot legitimately presuppose a controversial point that is central to deciding a claim; one must make a case for it. Before so doing, more conceptual analysis would be necessary: one must get a clear notion of personhood in order to establish common ground.

The more sophisticated "abortion is murder" anti-abortionist might agree that, under the approach just above, calling abortion "murder" is indeed hyperbole that hinders our understanding rather than aiding it. But he or she might also contend that we have mistakenly analyzed "murder" by linking the concept to its "dictionary definition." According to this view, murder is properly a moral issue, and moral law prohibits killing by abortion; hence, killing by abortion is unlawful. Whether this is correct or not must be decided by examining the cases made for and against it. (One consideration: a move from the ordinary concept that has been incorporated into civil law to a concept in moral law would open a whole range of new problems. We have a relatively clear, objective idea of what civil law prohibits and what it allows. Our understanding of moral law is much more contentious, especially when it comes to abortion.)

Clearly, then, one cannot justifiably accept or reject any claim without first understanding what the claim truly amounts to, and so the relevant concepts must be clearly laid out and rigorously adhered to from the outset. That is, the first step in justificatory reasoning will always be to "get clear" on relevant concepts (and what words will be used to express them).

IX   Conceptual Analysis

In order to zero in on a concept, it often pays to begin with a clear-cut, unambiguous case, then to try to figure out what features make it such a clear example. We call such clear-cut cases **paradigm cases**. Suppose, for instance, we are trying to understand the concept *violation* *of the public trust.* We might say: "Well, when a Congressman puts a person on his tax-supported payroll solely to keep that person on call to supply sexual favors, that's a violation of the public trust or I don't know what is." Now we have a paradigm to work with. Would it make any difference if the person were kept for the purpose mentioned but were paid from private funds? Would it be different if the person also performed genuine, job-related duties that someone had to do—type, answer phones, research issues? And so on. As we identify the essential characteristics of the paradigm case, we can begin to develop a generalized characterization of the concept at hand.

Borderline cases can also be very instructive in conceptual analysis. **Borderline cases** are ones about which we are not exactly sure whether or not they fall under a particular concept. By working on the fringes, one can often see what is essential and what is not. Is a person whose brain waves have ceased *dead* even if the heart still beats? Is a human fetus a *person?* ... a *citizen?* How about a human embryo or a human zygote? Is a person with 1,000 hairs on his head *bald?* Is Pluto a *planet?* Is a flying boat a *boat?* ... a *plane?* Does a hot stove *punish* the child who touches it? Is an untruth told in order to protect the life of a loved one a *lie?* How about an untruth told to protect the innocence of a child? Are "white lies" really *lies?* Is a dolphin a *fish?* Can a *patriot* refuse to serve his country in the military? Could an *omnipotent* (all powerful) *being* make a stone so big that he or she could not move it?

Cases such as these help us zero in on the salient features of the concepts that concern us.

3. REASON

I Reasons

Reasons are strange beasts. You can give a reason…and yet still have it. (In this way, reasons are like head colds but unlike apples.) Or you can give me your reason and, as a result, I have a reason…but the reason I have is not the one you gave me. You can (as with reputations) give a reason even though the reason you give isn't yours. Indeed, you can (as with headaches) give a reason even if you yourself don't have one.

Strange though they may be, reasons are crucial to both justification and persuasion. Whatever position you defend, that position is no better than the reason(s) supporting it. Reasons may come in the form of factual statements (i.e., descriptive claims), definitions (i.e., explication of concepts), or statements of principle. But no statement of fact, definition, or principle is by itself a reason. Such a statement becomes a **reason** when and only when it serves as an essential element in an argument.

II Argument

In the present context, we do not think of arguments as disputes between or among persons. Rather, we understand an **argument** to be a series of statements (also called *claims*). Among these statements, one or more **premises** provide the foundation that, through one or more logical **inferences**, leads to the **conclusion**. The premises state reasons; the conclusion states the position. In an argument, every statement will either be a premise or will be *inferred* from other statements in it. We use argument as a basic tool to discover truth and to convince doubters.

Disputes can be thought of as a sequence of arguments presented in support of conflicting positions. One individual can present an argument; disputes normally involve two or more individuals, each presenting their positions.

When we are serious about finding truth or gaining understanding, arguments are best presented in full detail so that they can be fairly and properly evaluated. Too often, people don't bother to put forth clear arguments. Rather, they are satisfied to hint at a lurking possible argument. This rudely forces the "audience" to do a major part of the arguer's job. As the audience, we recognize the suggestion of an argument by the presence of certain marker words or phrases: "since," "because," and "given that" often mark premises; "therefore," "thus," "hence," "consequently," "and so," "it follows that," "we find that," and "we conclude that" often mark conclusions.

Because well-founded, well-reasoned arguments are the primary tools by which claims—especially normative claims—are justified, it pays to master the art of argumentation.

III   Premises

What makes a good argument?

Unless an argument has an interesting conclusion, nobody cares. For this reason, an interesting conclusion is one element of a good argument; beyond that, the important elements are solid premises and tight reasoning.

First, let's consider **premises**. As already noted, premises are the foundation upon which a position must stand or fall. Unless one accepts all the relevant premises, one will certainly not agree to the conclusion—even if that conclusion follows necessarily from the premises. (That is why arguments based on authority or on scripture so often fail to convince.) Since no argument will convince anyone who does not accept its foundation, the practical test is always whether your audience accepts the premises without qualification. If not, there is no common ground and your argument has already failed.

Premises may lay out **concepts**, **factual claims**, or **principles**. Each of these realms has its own standard of acceptability: We have already seen that the first step in settling a dispute is to agree on the concepts (and the words to name those concepts). Often, a concept will itself become encapsulated in a definitional premise. Obviously, such premises must be clearly stated so the question "what does this mean?" cannot reasonably arise.

Non-definitional premises—that is, statements asserting fact or principle—should be true. (No rational person would build a position based on falsehood.) But truth itself won't make a premise worthy. Why not? Consider the statements: "Socrates had type O blood" and "Socrates did not have type O blood." One of these is certainly true, but neither would make a satisfactory premise because we have no reasonable basis upon which to believe either statement over the other. To reach common ground, premises themselves need to be well supported and reasonably believed by the intended audience.

Ultimately, you want premises that command acceptance not only by your intended audience, but also by any (thoughtful) person who encounters them. Factual premises that are quickly and easily verified by objective, empirical means, preferably by anyone with the will to do so, are particularly good in this respect. (But be careful, many empirical claims—urban myths and gossip, for instance—are widely believed but false.) For factual premises that are not so easily self-verified, you should (especially in written work) provide your audience with reference links to published studies in the scholarly literature (or, perhaps, to standard textbooks). Such references allow the reader to trace a claim back to common ground.

The most contentious premises typically are those that state principles. This is especially so in normative arguments: it is in the realm of principle that failure to establish common ground is most likely to occur. To find common ground, look for principles to which the question "why?" seems absolutely inappropriate...or even impertinent.[1] Thus, for example, in response to the claim that waste is bad or that a mature, rational person should, in general, have the right to decide what is or is not done to his or her body, most would find it exceedingly odd to ask "why?" Admittedly, this is a loose and somewhat subjective standard, but it does serve as a decent guideline for finding common-ground principles.

---

1. I owe this standard to William F. Baxter in *People or Penguins: The Case for Optimal Pollution* (Columbia University Press, 1974).

Finding workable premises is often the most challenging part of constructing a compelling and insightful argument. Folks naturally want to start with "high-level" premises. These may not be easily accepted. The trick is to find very basic and compelling principles that establish common ground and build upon them.

IV   Inferences

Just as the methodologies of empirical observation provide the tools by which we justify descriptive claims, conceptual analysis and argument provide the tools by which we justify normative claims. We judge how well a position is justified by considering the quality of the argument or arguments supporting it. We judge the quality of an argument based not only upon the clarity and defensibility of its premises but equally upon the merits of the logical reasoning involved. Hence, we must now look at reasoning.

Inferences are crucial to logical reasoning. An **inference** is the move to a statement that presumably *follows* from one or more prior statements.[2] Inferences are commonly sorted into two categories, **inductive** and **deductive**.

What's the difference?

Household dictionaries often say that inductive inferences move from the specific to the general, whereas deductive inferences move from the general to the specific. This won't do, however, because some deductive inferences move from specific to general,[3] and some inductive inferences move from general to specific.[4] Elementary math books may say that deductive reasoning is based upon facts and/or rules,

---

2. The term "inference" may also apply to the inferred statement itself.

3. Deductive, specific to specific: This animal is a cat; therefore (trivially) this animal is a cat. Deductive, specific to general: God is the only possible self-existent being; therefore, all possible self-existent beings are identical with God. Deductive, general to general: Horses are animals; therefore horses' heads are animals' heads.

4. Inductive, general to general: Cameras are like human eyes; human eyes have central blind spots; therefore cameras have central blind spots. Inductive, general to specific: Cars from this manufacturer start very reliably; therefore, this car will start the next time I try to start it. Inductive, specific to specific: Swan #1 is white; swan #2 is white; swan #3 is white; therefore swan #4 will be white.

whereas inductive reasoning is based on patterns. This gives a vague intuitive feeling, but little clarity: Rules are themselves pattern-based, and much (if not most) inductive reasoning starts with specific facts. In short, the distinction seems muddled. We can begin to clear it up by turning to a related notion: validity.

V   Validity

What does it mean for an inferred statement to *follow* from other statements? The fact that we use inferences with the hope of moving from known truths to unknown ones provides a clue: We want inferences that preserve truth, not ones that take us from truth to falsehood. The most desirable inferences, therefore, would be those for which *it would be **impossible** simultaneously for the premises to be true and the conclusion false.* In such cases an inference is said to be **valid**. (An argument in which all inferences are valid is also said to be valid.)

How can we determine whether an inference is valid or not?

VI   Form

Consider an argument sometimes put forward by animal rights activists:

3.1   If animals can suffer pain, then animals deserve moral
        consideration.
3.2   Animals can suffer pain.
Therefore,
3.3   Animals deserve moral consideration.

Now, one might deny the truth of 3.1; one might even deny the truth of 3.2; but one must admit that if 3.1 and 3.2 were both true, 3.3 would have to be true also. The key lies in the phrase "if…, then ___." That phrase, and phrases such as "it is not the case that…," "both…and ___," "either…or ___," along with the expressions "each…is such that ___," "some…is such that ___," "exactly one…is

such that____," and "...is identical with____," provide a logical frame-
work to our language and thinking. It can be demonstrated that certain formal structures in language—structures that depend upon these
expressions—will always preserve truth (assuming truth is present to
begin with). In other words, validity—that is, truth preservingness—is
a function of form alone.

Formalists seek to capture these structures by using letters of the
alphabet to abbreviate names or sentences. Thus, for example, we
might specify the following **scheme of abbreviations**:

> P: Animals can suffer pain.
> Q: Animals deserve moral consideration.

We may then use these **abbreviations** in the animal rights argument
mentioned above, uniformly replacing "animals can suffer pain" and
"animals deserve moral consideration" with "P" and "Q" respectively.
The result is:

> 3.1'   If P, then Q
> 3.2'   P
> Therefore,
> 3.3'   Q

Now, here's the interesting thing: pick any statements whatsoever, and
assign "P" and "Q" as their abbreviations. Next, stick those sentences
in the "stencil" just above, and the inference will be just as good as the
one in the animal rights argument. This form of inference is so common, it has been given a name: *modus ponens*. *Modus ponens* is just
one of many inference forms guaranteed to preserve truth. Some more
are listed in Appendices A and B. These structures are fundamental
to reasoning and have been "built into" English; if you understand
English, you understand these forms. Still, it pays both to focus on the
most important ones to help you keep them in mind, and to recognize
and to use them in your argumentation.

It is important to recognize that the truth or falsehood of the
premises is independent of the validity of any argument. Validity
guarantees that we do not go from truth to falsehood; it does not
guarantee truth. (If you start with a falsehood, you cannot go from
truth to falsehood.) Thus, an argument can be valid even if one or
more premises happen to be false. When evaluating arguments, we
must evaluate the truth of the premises independently of validity. If

the premises are true, however, validity assures us that the conclusion will also be true.

A valid argument with only true premises is said to be **sound**. Arguments that are strongly believed to be sound obviously establish strong justifications.

VII   Invalidity

Using valid inferences from common-ground premises is a good way to support one's position. Conversely, a solid way to criticize a position is to show that at least one of the inferences leading to it is not valid. How might one do this? Since a valid inference can never take us from truth to falsehood, and since validity is a function of form alone, finding a parallel inference where the premises are true and the conclusion is false will suffice to show that the original inference is **invalid**. The technique of abbreviation and fleshing out illustrated above can be very useful in this regard. Let's look at an example. Suppose someone proposes the following:

> 3.4   If Pat thinks life is meaningless, then Pat commits suicide.
> 3.5   Pat commits suicide.
> Therefore,
> 3.6   Pat thinks life is meaningless.

Is this argument valid? Using obvious abbreviations, we can schematize it as

> 3.4'   If P, then Q   )
> 3.5'   Q   )
> Therefore,   ) [INVALID INFERENCE]
> 3.6'   P   )

To show that this reasoning is not valid, we can imagine a clear, cold winter's day and flesh out the above using the following scheme of abbreviations:

> P: It is snowing.
> Q: It's cold outside.

The result is:

> 3.4″   If it is snowing, then it's cold outside.
> 3.5″   It's cold outside.
> Therefore,
> 3.6″   It is snowing.

But notice that on a crisp, clear winter's day, 3.4″ and 3.5″ are true and 3.6″ is false. This **counter example** shows that the conclusion does not follow from the premises. We know that the conclusion does not follow because we have seen that it is possible for the premises to be true while the conclusion is false. The schematized argument is invalid. (This particular form of bad reasoning is known as the *fallacy of affirming the consequent*.)

Here is another example of an invalid inference:

> 3.4   If Pat thinks life is meaningless, then Pat commits suicide.
> 3.7   Pat does not think life is meaningless.
> Therefore,
> 3.8   Pat does not commit suicide.

To show its invalidity, (and using "NOT" as an abbreviation for "it is not the case that") we note that this argument has the form:

> 3.4′   If P, then Q   )
> 3.7′   NOT P   )
> Therefore,   ) [INVALID INFERENCE]
> 3.8′   NOT Q   )

Fleshing the schema out with the same abbreviations we used above, we get the following counter example:

> 3.4″   If it is snowing, then it's cold outside.
> 3.7″   It's not snowing.
> Therefore,
> 3.8″   It is not cold outside.

Again, on a clear, cold day, 3.4″ and 3.7″ will be true while 3.8″ will be false. The purported conclusion does not follow from the premises; hence, the inference is invalid. (This particular form is called the *fallacy of denying the antecedent*.)

VIII   Counter Examples

We have seen, in a rather formal way, how a counter example can show that an inference is invalid. Counter examples, however, are not restricted to formal contexts. In general, a **counter example** is a *specific case* that demonstrates either the falsehood of a general claim or the invalidity of an inference or argument.

Here's a simple example of showing falsehood: Suppose someone were to assert that no individual can make a difference in this world. You might cite Jesus of Nazareth, Adolf Hitler, or Martin Luther King, Jr., as counter examples, that is, as individuals who have profoundly affected world history. In this way, counter examples can be very useful tools in attacking premises.

As we have said, validity is a matter of form alone. A valid inference is one in which it is impossible for the premises to be true and the conclusion false. Hence, to show that an argument is invalid, it suffices to produce an exactly parallel argument in which the premise or premises are clearly true and the conclusion is clearly false. This can be done either formally (as above) or informally. Consider, for example, the following argument:

3.9   A woman who consents to sexual intercourse knows full well that she risks pregnancy.

3.10   Therefore, a woman who consents to sexual intercourse must consent to any consequent pregnancy.

But surely this conclusion doesn't follow; look at the following exactly parallel argument:

3.9'   A woman who leaves the protection of her home knows full well that she risks sexual assault.

3.10'   Therefore, a woman who leaves the protection of her home must consent to any consequent sexual assault.

In arguments such as the one directly above, a counter example may help us identify a suppressed premise…one that may be false. In this case, for example, the suppressed premise seems to be the general principle that one must willingly accept every known potential consequence of every action, with no right to correct or even to try to prevent whatever happens. But that's just goofy.

As you can see, the counter example is a powerful tool for correcting error, focusing on presuppositions, and clarifying concepts.

IX Induction

A number of really interesting arguments fail to be valid in the sense we have described above. For them, the truth of the premises is not sufficient to guarantee the truth of the conclusion. Such arguments are often categorized as **inductive**. Given true premises, an inductive inference can warrant belief that the conclusion is probably true. Inferences (and arguments) that provide such warrant are said to be powerful, strong, or **cogent**.

Though cogent arguments cannot provide the very strong justifications that sound arguments do, they are often the best we can do...and they can provide solid justifications for our positions.

The most common sorts of inductive inferences involve **abstraction** (extracting common features from a set of specific examples), **generalization** (formulating general concepts based on a collection of instances), **abduction** (inference to the best or most probable explanation), or **analogy** (inference to an unobserved similarity in cases where a number of observed similarities are present). (Abduction is the sort of reasoning that Sherlock Holmes mistakenly called "deduction"; it is reasoning to the most probable explanation.)

The variety of useful inductive inferences is too great to sketch out in the way we have done in Appendix B for deductive inferences. Inductive inference is something of a creative enterprise. In ETHICS, we often consider a particular act or set of acts that seem particularly praiseworthy or particularly abhorrent and try to generalize or abstract an underlying principle that appears to account for this status. Analogies can also play an important role in ethical thinking. Parallels between something we understand well and something we don't understand well can give us insights into the unknown. Every analogy carries disanalogy[5] as baggage, however, and one must always be careful in extending the analogical parallels.

---

5. Here "analogy" refers to the comparison of two distinct things that are similar (analogous) in many respects but are not identical in kind and accordingly have dissimilarities as well; these dissimilarities comprise a disanalogy.

In one way or another, every type of argument crops up in ETHICS. Often the conclusions of one argument become premises in another. Sometimes a set of arguments will work inductively from specific cases to general principles. Those principles may then serve as premises in deductive arguments. Much of ethical analysis comprises critical inquiry into the probability of the premises and the quality of the reasoning in the arguments. In one sense, ETHICS is all about the arguments: Are the premises (reasons) clearly understood and universally accepted as true? Is the reasoning beyond question? If so, the conclusion presents a solid ethical position.

X Deductive Form

In Section IV, we noticed some difficulties with the usual ways of differentiating between deductive and inductive inferences. Let's take another look.

Some logic references say that a deductive argument is exactly the same as a valid argument. But this characterization also presents difficulties. We quite naturally use "valid" and "invalid" as modifiers of "deductive argument." If the terms *valid* and *deductive* were indeed synonymous, "valid deductive argument" would be synonymous with "valid valid argument," an uninformative redundancy. Similarly, the expression "invalid deductive inference" would be the equivalent of "invalid valid inference"...and that's pure nonsense.

It seems that if we equate "valid" and "deductive," "deductive" becomes useless and we may as well strike it from our vocabulary. Actual usage, however, suggests that "valid" and "deductive" are not synonymous. The term "deductive" seems somehow to be related to the appearance or manner of presentation of an argument or inference. Any inference or argument that contains premises rich in the vocabulary that provides logical structure—"if..., then___," "it is not the case that...," "both...and___," "either...or___," "each...is such that___," "some...is such that___," "exactly one...is such that___," "...is identical with___," and so on—and that is marked by the sort of step-by-step form that valid arguments must take, or that seems to have been presented with the intent and expectation that the inferences are valid, will be recognized as deductive. That is, in ordinary usage, a deductive inference is one that either resembles the form that a valid argument takes or else purports to present a conclusion that follows necessarily from the premises. By contrast, an inference will be seen as inductive if it either lacks the deductive vocabulary or if it is presented as one that purports only to yield a conclusion that follows probabilistically, not necessarily.

For our purposes, the important point lies not with the terminology, but rather with the success or failure to achieve what is purported. *A successful deductive argument guarantees the preservation of truth, whereas a successful inductive argument allows for the possibility that we may slip from truth to falsehood.* Hence, after determining whether the premises are true, and whether the argument is successful, we must remember that an inductive argument gives less rigorous support to our position than a deductive one does. When defending a position with inductive arguments, then, we should be especially mindful of our fallibility (and perhaps maintain an extra degree of humility).

A final point on a slightly different path: You can always recast an inductive inference into the form of an "if...then___" statement.[6] Using such statements as premises, you can transform any argument into an argument in deductive form.

Why bother? The great virtue of putting an argument in full deductive form is that it forces one to make all the premises explicit. Sometimes an argument sounds good until it becomes apparent that some premise is necessary for the argument's validity but is itself sheer nonsense. This virtuous explicitness may be lacking when arguments take inductive form.

---

6. One does this by replacing the ellipses with the inductive premise (or a conjunction of the inductive premises) and, in addition, by replacing the underlining with the inductive conclusion.

4. WISDOM AND UNDERSTANDING

How can one live a good life? We have set out to answer this central question by using our own wit and reason. In preparing to attack the question, we have tried to understand something of the scope and limits of wit and reason as a problem-solving tool. We have discussed *concept, fact,* and *reasoning.* We need now to address *principle* and mention some intellectual blunders that can derail us.

I Disputes

Generally speaking, people don't realize that there is a problem until a dispute arises. Then, interested parties who hold mutually conflicting views develop arguments to support their respective positions. Disputes can arise in both the normative and the descriptive realms. The characteristic difference between the two is that every argument about normative issues must contain at least one value claim or statement of normative principle, whereas arguments related purely to matters of empirical fact do not. Both sorts of argument will likely contain premises that make descriptive or factual claims. Both may contain premises that define concepts. And both will involve logical inferences.

Since arguments may incorporate concepts, facts, principles, and logic, disagreements may spring from any of these. In any normative matter, the normative element ordinarily will be embodied in a principle. Thus, when disagreements arise, the source may be any one of four kinds: conceptual, factual, normative, or logical. Sometimes disputes appear to be about ethical matters but actually turn out to be about facts, or about concepts, or even about the legitimacy of the logical inferences made in the argument.

Often, then, the best first step towards settling a dispute is to figure out exactly where the disagreement originates. This may seem obvious, but surprisingly many disputes that might be easily resolved remain unsettled because people argue about facts or norms when the central problem is one of concepts or logic.

Consider, for example, a case where some deranged person, "DP," wants to kill someone whose location you know. DP has you tied up, puts a gun to your head, and threatens to "blow your brains out" unless you tell where the intended victim is. Should you, as a moral person, tell DP the location?

One consideration seemingly in favor of telling is the normative principle: you should not lie.

Some might object to this principle. It is usually wrong to lie, they might say, *but not when you are under duress—and especially not when truth-telling could lead to murder!* Indeed, this is a case where a moral person definitely ought to lie, and the principle needs to be modified accordingly.

On the other hand, one might unquestioningly accept the principle that one should not lie, but suggest that telling an untruth to DP would not be a lie. The person who wants to modify the normative principle has understood that lies are untruths, but may have failed to see that not all untruths are lies. Fiction is made up entirely of untruths, but these untruths are not lies. Does one lie if one utters only truths but those truths mislead the listener? In a negotiation, is a bluff a lie? What exactly is a lie? It's those pesky concepts again! Before we can decide on the moral principle, we need to get clear on the concept.[1]

II   Principle

Normative and factual relationships show up in arguments as general claims of principle. One of the important uses of argument is to find solid general principles for premises. Often the best way to find

---

1. Whether a lie occurs seems somehow tied to what legitimate expectations the hearer has regarding truth and whether he or she does or does not have a right to know the information in question. The exact details of the link between these rights and expectations need to be worked out.

such premises is through the inductive process of generalization from specific, paradigm cases. Given a paradigm case, we ask ourselves, "What is the underlying principle here?"

Persons who are adamantly opposed to aborting pregnancy, for example, almost always agree that an exception arises in cases where the mother's life is in danger. In such cases, they say, abortion is morally acceptable.

What general principle underlies this exception? The answer seems to be the prima facie[2] moral right to self-defense. Generally speaking, any person whose life is threatened has a moral right to take whatever steps might be necessary to end that threat; this is a very strong moral right, which permits one to take the life of another person or persons if that is required in order to defend oneself. This right comes as close as any to being recognized and accepted by all moral theories. Under this principle, then, if pregnancy poses a threat to the mother's life, she has a moral right to defend herself against that threat by having an abortion.

Here's another example: Sometimes persons who advocate a return to formal prayer in civic forums cite the fact that many of our founding fathers referred to God in their writings and led prayer in civic forums. Therefore, these persons conclude, we may do likewise. For the argument to work, we must accept the principle that it is acceptable for us to do whatever our founding fathers did. But suppose this principle were correct. By it, since many of our founding fathers owned slaves, it would be OK for us to own slaves today. Of course, slavery is not acceptable: the principle fails, and so, therefore, does any argument that depends upon it.

This example illustrates the up and down flow of principled reasoning. We generalize and then we test the generalization.

Suppose someone asserts that capital punishment for convicted murderers is not morally acceptable. When the state executes a murderer, it does just what the murderer did: kills a person. By its action, the state condones killing. This sounds plausible until we consider what principle might underlie the contention: by doing to a criminal what the criminal did, we condone the crime. But by that principle, when the state incarcerates a kidnapper (holding him against his

---

2. Literally "first face"; hence clear, obvious, or apparent (though subject to possible correction upon further examination).

will), the state condones kidnapping. Of course, the state does just the opposite; the principle is foolish.

Premises that appear in deductive arguments are themselves commonly justified by inductive argument. It is in this way that we generalize to a principle, then test the principle.

III Abstraction

Abstraction, like generalization to principle, is a form of inductive inference. Abstraction can be a powerful tool, but we must be aware of its dangers.

We think with experience—more precisely, thought content traces back to what we have seen, felt, tasted, smelled, or heard. Several important points arise from this principle.

First, since original ideas are original only in the sense that they are the result of combining quite un-original ideas in an unusual way, thought demands broad experience. Furthermore, only wide experience enables us to understand our fellow man and our culture. (Hence, core distribution requirements in colleges and universities.) But most importantly, the principle points to problems that arise when we deal in abstractions. To abstract is to "tear away" from experience. Abstractions can be powerful tools of thought, provided they are supported by references to people, events, and things of experience. But abstractions can also be traps. Danger arises when abstract terms are employed without experience sufficient to fix their meaning. Misunderstanding and foolishness result.

The higher the degree of abstraction, the more is left out; hence, broader experience is necessary to give the abstraction real content. Consider, for instance, a certain object at which I can point. This object has an unlimited number of characteristics. When I look at or touch the object, I am one step removed from its full reality; I have already abstracted. Suppose I name the object "Elsie." Here I have left out all the qualities of the object. The name is not the thing. Indeed, you will understand me when I speak of Elsie only if you too have seen and touched her. When I have experienced a large number of objects (Elsie, Bossie, Bluebell, Cleo…) I may notice that in certain respects each resembles the others. I tear away from reality the abstract concept, *cow*. In so doing, I exclude most of what makes Elsie Elsie, Bossie Bossie, and so on. It is only by virtue of having experienced a number of cows that the concept *cow* has any content for me. With broader experience, I may be able to tear from reality what Elsie shares with chickens and pigs and goats: I form the concept *livestock*. When my experiences are so varied that I can tear from Elsie what she has in common with other livestock and tractors and barns and corn and cabbage and timber and oranges and so forth, the concept *farm assets* has content. Notice that, in each step of abstraction, more of Elsie is left out, and that broader experience is required to give the concept content. We could continue abstracting to *asset, wealth*, and so forth, but the point should be clear.

Because *words* for abstract concepts can be used without the experience necessary to give those concepts content, there is a great danger that we may replace understanding by word manipulation. You may get away in school with word manipulation even if you don't understand the words you use. But you can never achieve wisdom unless each concept you use is well founded in experience. Thus, a good practice is always to illustrate abstract principles with one or more "concrete" examples—that is, examples of very low-degree abstraction. This will assure you that you understand what you are talking about, and it will also increase the chances that your interlocutors will understand you too.

IV Fit

An excellent way to help us understand a problem is to consider related concepts. Understanding *knowledge*, for example, will be aided by also considering *belief, truth, evidence*, and so on. *Freedom* becomes clearer with an examination of *license, responsibility, determinism, choice*, and other concepts.

Similarly, the attempt to fit one claim in with others can help evaluate that claim. Years ago, scientists accounted for certain cases of combustion by claiming that the process involved the escape of a negative-weight substance (called "phlogiston") from the fuel. This claim fit nicely with two observations: (1) the ash-residue weighs more than the fuel; (2) there is a strong updraft during the process. The idea that phlogiston had negative weight, however, did not fit well with the observation that all other known substances were of positive weight. This incoherence was disturbing. Finally, it was shown that a process involving positive-weight oxygen could account for combustion phenomena. Phlogiston theorists switched over to the better-fitting oxygen theory.

It may be difficult to step back and spot related concepts or claims. Our contemporary fashion of narrow specialization fosters a tendency for people to pigeon-hole ideas, to develop a form of myopic tunnel vision for each concern. This semi-blindness allows individuals to ignore even striking incoherencies and to miss clear parallels. Thus, the church-goer does not let his religion interfere with his business; the teacher does not notice that the morning's headlines are a perfect illustration of today's lecture; the astrologer rejects belief in flying saucers and ghosts on the grounds that there is no evidence for them; and so forth.

To build wisdom, try always to put things in perspective with everything you know, then see how it all fits together.

V   Comparison and Investigation

In the main, we create arguments in order to justify a position, or to convince or persuade someone—even ourselves—of a point. But in addition to this, arguments can be used for other interesting purposes. When we can't tell whether a position is strictly right or wrong, for example, we can often use argument to figure out which of two competing positions is stronger.

Also, we can use arguments to "investigate" a hypothesis: we draw out logical consequences to see where the hypothesis leads. This can lead to important insights. (If you are familiar with the Platonic dialogues, you will recognize the masterful way Socrates used argument as an investigatory tool.) If the argument takes us to a contradiction, we know that at least one of our premises must be false—how do we know this?—and if we were careful about all our other premises, we can rightly suspect that the hypothesis is the culprit. (This is the technique used in the classic argument[3] based

---

3. If an all-knowing, all-loving, all-powerful god exists, the world would be free of evil. But the world is anything but free of evil! Therefore, an all-knowing, all-powerful, all-loving god does not exist.

on the existence of evil, which purports to show that an all-loving, all-knowing, all-powerful god cannot exist.)

VI   Common Blunders

There are a number of blunders that crop up in arguments. Here are some of the more common ones:

Equivocation. Conceptual confusion often manifests itself in equivocation. A little joke illustrates the idea:

> Jo: Man, the carpet burn on my knee really smarts.
> Mo: You could use some smarts! Can you get a carpet burn on your head?

Equivocations occur when a word switches meanings. Arguments that turn on equivocation fail because equivocation changes the subject in midstream, so to speak. Consider an argument like this one:

> No child should have to work for a living.
> Every person is someone's child.
> Therefore, no person should have to work for a living.

Here the switch in meaning between *young person* and *offspring* stands out so strongly that no one will likely be misled. Equivocation can, however, be quite subtle and difficult to spot. This partially accounts for the persistence of some widely recited arguments regarding abortion that depend for their plausibility upon equivocations among the meanings of "person," "life," "human being," "kill," and "murder." Failure to identify and eliminate hidden equivocation may well be one of the most pervasive blunders around.

Question Begging. To "beg the question" is to assume that which needs to be proven. Sometimes this happens when one draws inferences that depend upon some unstated, essential premise. Often, it happens when one poses a rhetorical question rather than building a case. Finally, it occurs when one offers a (sometimes not very well) disguised version of the conclusion as a premise in support of that conclusion, thus producing a "circular argument."

Consider, for example, the kind of reasoning one often hears reported when the stock market is making nice gains: "Stocks were up today on news of a jump in retail sales. Experts said that the sales jump occurred because consumers are happy and confident about their financial situation. That confidence traces directly to the sense of wealth consumers are feeling as rising stock prices boost the dollar value of their investment portfolios."

In other words: stocks are up because stocks are up!

Begging the question occurs with amazing frequency, especially in the normative realm. Of course, circularity seldom appears quite so clearly as in the stock market example. More likely, it slithers in, insidiously buried in long, convoluted arguments. Failure to realize that some unstated premise has been used and is essential happens all too often. Undergraduates particularly like the trick of using unanswered, rhetorical questions to avoid justification or elaboration of premises.

Be watchful for cases of question begging. To avoid it yourself, never leave a question unanswered, and be certain that your premises are based on something other than the conclusion you intend them to support.

Jumping the Fact-Value Gap. In the eighteenth century, David Hume gave fame to the point that one cannot derive a normative claim from solely factual ones without some premise that explicitly links the two realms. To jump from an *is* (a fact) to an *ought* (a value) without such a premise is to jump the fact-value gap. Such a jump is a special case of begging the question and is never valid. Premises that link fact and value are, as we have said, particularly contentious. In the early twentieth century, British philosopher G. E. Moore (1873–1978) contended that certain normative terms (*goodness* for example) are (like *yellow*) primitive and cannot be defined. He called the attempt to define such terms using only descriptive language the **"Naturalistic Fallacy."**[4] If Moore was correct about this limitation on definition, to commit the Naturalistic Fallacy would be to jump the fact-value gap. If Moore was mistaken about the limitation, a definitional premise (rather than a linking principle) might perhaps bridge the fact-value gap.

Diversions. Diversions can be of two sorts. Either an issue is simply ignored and replaced by another (as when the anti-evolutionist mocks

---

4. *Principia Ethica* (1903).

the real issues by asking if anyone really believes that the chimpanzee is his grandfather), or else a weak argument is substituted for a strong one and the weak argument is attacked. We might, for instance, claim that our only reason not to steal is that we were taught as children not to, and then proceed to point out that the same applied to our parents and their parents before them, ad infinitum. The conclusion, that there really isn't any good reason not to steal, is possible only because concerns such as morality or the fact of possible fines or imprisonment are ignored. A "straw man" has been defeated, but the straw man is a diversion from the interesting and important issues.

Presuppositions. In March 1967, President Lyndon Johnson was asked whether he was searching for a successor to our ambassador in Saigon, Henry Cabot Lodge. "No, there is no truth that I am looking for a successor," the president responded. Less than a week later, Ellsworth Bunker was named to replace Lodge. The press was livid, but the president had been absolutely accurate: he was not *looking* for a successor, he had *already found* one. The newsmen were duped owing to a certain false presupposition they had made: they took "not looking" to mean "not replacing."

A presupposition amounts to an underlying condition or assumption that is implicitly imposed, often without recognition. Presuppositions are easier to spot in questions than anywhere else. But whenever they appear, they are likely to be buried in adjectives or adverbs. "Do you *still* beat your wife?" presupposes that wife-beating has occurred. "What is your stand on the *immoral* profits that industry X is raking in?" presupposes that X is making some sort of profits and that it is somehow immoral to do so. "Are you with us or against us?" presupposes that a position of neutrality is not possible. And so on.

False presuppositions are a major cause of confusion and a major tool of deception. Do not allow yourself to be duped. Advances almost always result when presuppositions are identified, made explicit, and examined on their own merits (or lack thereof).

VII Using the Tools

We have focused so far on our natural abilities to perceive and understand—our wit—and on our powers of reasoning. We have done so in order to bring the rudiments of critical thinking[5] and problem solving under our command. Let us now apply these skills by examining five pairs of core normative concepts. What do these concepts really amount to? To whom or what do they apply? Can we account for their origins?

Let's find out.

---

5. ROOTS OF SELECTED NORMATIVE PREDICATES

Every man by natural passion, calleth that good which pleaseth him for the present, or so far forth as he can forsee; and in like manner, that which displeaseth him, bad.[1]
—Thomas Hobbes, *De Corpore Politico* [1650]
(Molesworth IV, 109)

I Good and Bad

In the epigraph to this chapter, Thomas Hobbes (1588–1679) simply observes that the predicate "is good" and the predicate "is bad" express, respectively, the satisfaction and frustration of wants or desires.

If you are not immediately convinced that Hobbes' observation is correct, imagine a universe exactly like ours except that it has no living thing (not even a god) in it. In such a world, nothing is good and nothing is bad; the concepts of **good** and **bad** have no application.[2]

---

1. Owing to changes in meaning over time, 350-year-old English has effectively become a foreign language. Hobbes used "evil," but I have translated it to "bad" because that word better captures contemporary usage.

2. G. E. Moore famously contended that things like goodness and beauty exist independently of minds: even if no minds are present, he claimed, a beautiful world would be better than a horribly ugly one; a world filled with goodness would be better than one filled with evil. The following discussion is of the predicate "is good" (not the predicate "exhibits goodness"), and as the "is" is one of predication, not identity or composition, it need not be seen as taking a stand on the ontological status of goodness.

Now, add one living being, but let it be a creature governed solely and completely by reason. A bit of thought about this world makes it apparent (1) that such a creature would not long survive, and (2) that the predicates "is good" and "is bad" still don't apply. A purely rational creature would not long survive because, being governed solely and completely by reason, it would totally lack wants and desires. Having no wants or desires, it would have no *motive* to do anything whatsoever. Perhaps it could reason out what would be necessary to survive, but lacking any desire to assuage hunger (for example), it would seek no nourishment. Wants or desires are necessary (though not sufficient) for (voluntary) action.

If we now imagine that sole inhabitant to be a **conative** being—a being who has wants and desires—normative qualities instantly arise. These qualities can be expressed by the predicates "is good" and "is bad." Our creature regards that which fulfills a desire as good and that which frustrates a desire as bad.[3]

Over the years, through metaphor, analogy, and so forth, the words "good" and "bad" have taken on additional grammatical roles and variant meanings, but the root meaning remains as described by Hobbes: Anything that satisfies a want or desire is good; anything that frustrates a want or desire is bad. As wants and desires are relative to the individual, so good and bad are relative to the individual—what's good or bad for one may or may not be good or bad for another—and the individual is the sole and ultimate arbiter.

What "justifies" one's wants and desires? Think back to the earliest times of the human species. Imagine two persons. One likes having sexual intercourse; the other finds it painful and unpleasant. Which of these, do you suppose, is more likely to be your ancestor? Or think of two individuals: One loves the bitter taste of strychnine and hates sweet things; the other gags on bitter things but loves the sweet taste of things like nuts and berries. Which do you suppose is more likely to be your ancestor?

Babies are born liking sweet and disliking bitter; this disposition is built into their genes. Indeed, apparently our most basic likes and dislikes are all genetically based. Hence, the "justification" for calling something good or bad traces to the fact that God or Nature gave us a genetic grounding for basic likes and dislikes, and those likes and dislikes determine what's good or bad.

---

3. I owe the above account of connation to Richard Taylor.

II   Right and Wrong

Returning once more to examine our imaginary universe, we notice that the predicates "is right" and "is wrong" do not yet apply. Suppose, however, that we add a number of conative beings who interact with each other. Eventually, specific social practices will evolve. These evolve naturally because most inhabitants regard each practice as bringing about something good. For example: I am approached by a stranger. I am fearful. Will I be attacked? Ah! The stranger extends his fully open, weapons-holding hand. He is unarmed. I need not fear an attack. That is *good*! I reciprocate. The stranger's thoughts parallel mine. We shake hands. The practice of shaking hands arises because the vast majority of persons who encounter the practice see it as good. That is, shaking hands is "justified" by virtue of the fact that it is a **common good**, meaning that it satisfies some desire that is common to (nearly) all persons and so (nearly) everyone thinks it is good.

Simple practices such as shaking hands become captured in informal, unwritten, often unspoken, **rules** of social behavior. It **is wrong** to break these rules. It **is right** to follow them. The predicates "is right" and "is wrong," then, are tied to following or breaking rules. As it turns out, this tie goes beyond social practices. If you follow the rules of addition, for example, the sum you obtain will be right. If you do not follow the rules, your sum will be wrong.

Two ancillary concepts worth mentioning crop up at this point: **praiseworthy** and **blameworthy**. The social tool for encouraging us to follow the rules (and do what's right) is praise. Blame serves to discourage breaking the rules (and doing what's wrong).

As with the words "good" and "bad," "right" and "wrong" have taken on additional meanings, but the root meaning is clearly rule-related.

III   Legal and Illegal

When societies become formally organized and institute governments, legislative bodies (councils, commissions, legislatures) and courts formalize rules and publish them in written form. These rules are called

laws. Governments use their power to enforce laws and to compel citizens to obey them, or to punish them if they don't. The predicates "is legal" and "is illegal" apply respectively to that which is in accord with law and that which is forbidden by it.

Along with the predicates "is legal" and "is illegal," a number of interesting notions arise with the appearance of government. A **citizen** is one who is a member of the body politic, who owes allegiance to its government, and has a right to the benefits provided by its government. The courts comprise a system in which judgments are made. The system is accordingly called "judicial" and gives rise to the predicates "is just" and "is unjust." It **is just** to receive that to which one is due by law; it **is unjust** to be denied what is due by law. **Legal standing** (*locus standi*) concerns whether one has sufficient connection to the law to be entitled to have the courts decide an action on its merits. In effect, the law applies only to those who have standing.

Here also, we first find **duty**. As Hobbes put it: "To follow what is prescribed by law, is duty…" (*Philosophical Rudiments*, 1647, 1651; Molesworth II, 183). The root notion of doing one's duty is tied to the notion of law. (This will turn out to be important when we examine Kant's ethical theory.) Correlative with the idea of a duty is the idea of a right. (Notice, "right" in this context is a noun, not a predicate.) A **right** is a warranted claim against someone (or some organization). For every right, then, there must be a reciprocal duty; someone (or some organization) must have a duty to satisfy the claim. Similarly, for every duty, there must be a reciprocal right.

What "justifies" any given law? One might first think that the only justification needed is that the law be created through due legislative process by those whom a social contract empowers to make law. This won't quite do, however. The legislature may overstep its legitimate power as defined by the social contract (formally expressed in the United States by the Constitution). In addition, not all law is **statutory**. So-called **common law** originates independently of the legislature; it grows solely through decisions of the courts, and this gives us a hint as to what legitimizes law. When there is no legislative guidance, courts use a standard known as **compelling public interest** to justify their findings. The general idea is that any specific law must be either necessary to the preservation of, or of significant benefit to, the society *as a whole*, not merely to some individuals within the society. Furthermore, that benefit must be so great as to overwhelm the costs from any restriction on individual liberty or other harm that the law might carry with it.[4]

IV   Ethical and Unethical

As we have said, the Greeks originated the philosophical study of ethics. Cicero (106–43 B.C.E.), the Roman statesman and man of letters who translated much Greek philosophy into Latin, coined the word *moralis* (from *mores*, meaning "customs" or "conventions") to translate the Greek *ethikos* (which was originally coined from *ethos*, meaning "customs" or "conventions"). The English words "ethics" and "morals" come from the respective Greek and Latin, and have traditionally meant the same thing. In the past few decades, however, the pairs "is ethical / is unethical" and "is moral / is immoral" have taken on some differences.[5] "Ethical" and "unethical" have come to refer to behavior within identifiable affinity groups—usually professional groups.[6] Thus, we have journalistic ethics, medical ethics, business ethics, legal ethics, education ethics, financial ethics, corporate ethics, and so on. In many cases, codes of ethics for the members of the group are published and presented to them by a **professional association** (the American Medical Association, for example). Often, boards or committees are empowered to investigate alleged ethical misdeeds and punish any offenders by fines, sanctions, or even restricting the ability to practice the profession. Such codes need not be limited to those produced by

---

4. This account of the justification for law is not entirely without controversy; the reader is referred to the great body of literature on political philosophy for alternative views. To this end, the search term "jurisprudence" is particularly relevant, but a more manageable starting point might be the *Stanford Encyclopedia of Philosophy* article on public justification at http://plato.stanford.edu/entries/justification-public/.

5. These differences may lead to confusions as a consequence of the associated nouns and adjectives holding mostly to their traditional usages. Thus, *ethics* still names the subject we study (though it might now more coherently be called *morality*), and correspondingly, we still use "ethical skepticism," for example, when "moral skepticism" would probably be more perspicuous.

6. This use of "ethics" reprises Greek usage prior to Socrates, focusing on the *ethike aretai*—traits of excellence—associated with *roles* in society (physician, soldier, herdsman, etc.). Socrates focused on the *ethike aretai* of *persons*.

large affinity organizations, however. Codes of ethics can also be promulgated by even the smallest individual company. The point to be noticed is that professional or affinity codes of ethics comprise sets of rules applying to those in the profession or group, and these rules may be enforced by sanctions from the affinity group.

In a straightforward sense, then, "is ethical" and "is unethical" have come to express conformity or disconformity with rules promulgated (and often enforced) by a particular profession or organization.

How these rules are to be justified and how they may be critiqued will be issues that we shall touch upon in subsequent chapters. As a practical matter, however, the ethical codes promulgated by professional bodies can be expected to take the interests of the profession itself as the most compelling factor. These interests often boil down to building and maintaining a monopoly on who will be allowed to practice the profession while at the same time encouraging sufficient competency (and whatever else is necessary) to enhance the general respectability and reputation of its practitioners.

V   Moral and Immoral

Like *right* and *wrong*, *legal* and *illegal*, and *ethical* and *unethical*, the concepts *moral* and *immoral* seem to be tied to rules. Moral rules, though they may be cataloged or even preached, are not normally enforced by some outside entity. Rather, if and when they are enforced, they are enforced internally by an individual's conscience.

What distinguishes *moral rules* from other rules?

After some thought about the concepts above, we realize that different levels of commitment accompany the different conceptual levels. Generally speaking, we feel a stronger sense of obligation with each move from *good/bad* to *right/wrong* to *legal/illegal* to *ethical/unethical* and to *moral/immoral*.

So, for example, on a very hot day, one might desire to shed one's clothing and splash around in the big fountain in front of city hall. In a word, splashing around in the nude would be *good*. But in our society, public nudity is a no-no. Thus splashing around in the nude would also be *wrong*. Wrong trumps good.

Or consider what happens when a judge orders a journalist to reveal sources used in a news story. By virtue of the judge's order, the journalist has a legal duty to reveal the information; however, journalistic ethics prohibits such a revelation. Here, journalistic ethics trumps civil law, and the good journalist will go to jail rather than divulge a source. Ethics trumps law.

Finally, suppose a patient reveals to her psychiatrist that she expects to eviscerate her boyfriend on Halloween. Ethics prohibits revealing medical information without the express consent of the patient.[7] Nevertheless, the psychiatrist will feel a compelling moral obligation to violate confidentially and inform the appropriate authorities so that they may act to prevent the crime. Morality trumps ethics.

These observations suggest the distinctive characteristic of morality: *Morality*, as distinct from all the other normative concepts discussed above, *encompasses our highest or strongest values*—the ones we will give up only after we have given up all others. Our highest values as individuals are central to our beings as individuals. They tell us who we are. They *define* who we are. As such, they are precious to us.

If you belittle, destroy, or trash something that is precious to me, you attack *who I am*. Such an attack angers me. The power of attacking strong values is almost beyond comprehension. It explains how cartoons published in Denmark can incite the burning of embassies halfway around the world. It accounts for the horror of hate crimes.

But when we say that morality has to do with our highest values, we understand the "our" to be *universal* and *collective*, not, like the editorial "we," a function of the individual. The ambit of morality comes from the set of highest values shared in common among all beings with moral standing.

It is worth noting that morality, ethicality, and legality all involve rules. This helps us explain everyday uses where "right" shows up in place of "legal," "ethical," or "moral," and "wrong" shows up in place of "illegal," "unethical," or "immoral." Here, "right" seems to be short for

---

7. The 1976 decision in *Tarasoff v. Regents of University of California* requires therapists to take "reasonable steps" to protect potential victims; it does not require breech of confidentiality.

"right legally," "right ethically," or "right morally," and "wrong" seems to be short for "wrong legally," "wrong ethically," or "wrong morally." These expressions, though they implicitly emphasize the place of rules, add nothing essential. Indeed, they are equivalent respectively to the simpler "legal," "ethical," "moral," "illegal," "unethical," and "immoral." Likewise, instances where "good" or "bad" are used in place of "right," "legal," "ethical," "moral," "wrong," "illegal," "unethical," or "immoral" work because whatever is right, legal, ethical, or moral will most commonly be seen as satisfying desires, whereas whatever is wrong, illegal, unethical, or immoral most commonly frustrates desires. Hence, it is not necessarily a strict misuse to employ "good" or "bad" or "right" or "wrong" in place of the words that carry stronger values; nevertheless, such usage dilutes the force and content of one's claim. For this reason, it is better avoided.

We should also note that the characterization of morality presented here helps us understand some of the great values-based conflicts of our day. Individuals, even large groups of individuals, may confuse their highest *personal* values—that is, a strong *good*—with the highest values of all humankind—that is, *morality*. That confusion may introduce a strong *sense* of moral value in the believer. That sense may be so strong that one will fight and even die for the value, believing such action to be a defense of morality. However, when the value is fundamentally personal, not universal, the value lacks moral grounding, no matter how much it may seem otherwise. (The same point can be made relative to confusions of merely social values with truly moral ones.)

Unlike good and bad, right and wrong, legal and illegal, and ethical and unethical—concepts that properly apply only to an individual or to a defined group—morality is understood to be universal. It applies uniformly to everyone, everywhere. Morality trumps everything else.

We may not always have the will to do what is moral, but we always feel that we have in some way been untrue to ourselves if we fail. What these highest (universal) values should be (or are) and how they may be justified is, in the end, what ETHICS as a discipline is all about. We can now turn to these matters.

Figure 5.1 outlines the main ideas in this chapter. It also includes a couple of concepts that will be introduced in later chapters.

Figure 5.1: The Core Normative "Ladder"

Predicates	"Root" link	Social level	"Justified" by	Correlative notions
is moral/is immoral	Rules [?]* for all persons [?]	universe	[justification not yet (fully) determined]	THE GOOD moral standing
is ethical/is unethical**	rules for professions, affinity groups	affinity groups	interests (or well-being) of affinity group	
is legal/is illegal	written rules enforced by government	the state, government	compelling public interest	rights, duties, justice, citizenship, legal standing
is right/is wrong	customs, informal rules	groups/ society	common good	social standing
is good/is bad	wants, desires; likes, dislikes	individual	genetics (via evolution or design)	

*This bracketed question mark appears in recognition of a slightly different perspective, one that approaches ETHICS as a study of virtues rather than of rules. Similarly, the second bracketed question mark recognizes the possibility that, as some would now argue, morality may apply to certain non-persons (including animals) or even to abstract entities such as the environment. Finally, the bracketed comment in the justification column reminds us that ethicists have not yet reached full agreement as to exact justification. The remaining chapters in this book address the possibilities.
**"Ethics" comes from Greek; "morals" comes from Latin. Originally, "ethics" and "morals" were synonymous.

6. ARISTOTLE

I THE GOOD

In the last chapter we discussed the predicate "is good." The word "good" can also be used as a noun or as an adjective. The meaning of the noun flows from that of the predicate. An object (or state of affairs) that satisfies (someone's) desire(s) is called "a good." We use this term commonly when we speak of merchants selling their goods.

Aristotle opens his *Nicomachean Ethics* by observing that goods may be thought of as the ends (outcome, conclusion, product) of art, inquiry, action, or pursuit. Thus, for example, a shoe would be the end of the cobbler's art. As there are many arts, inquiries, actions, and pursuits, there will be many ends. Even within a particular endeavor, there may be multiple ends, some of which may be subsidiary to others. Carpenters may, for example, build scaffolding so that masons can lay bricks for a weatherproof exterior to a dwelling being built as a home for a pair of newlyweds. The "chief good" here, the one for the sake of which the other goods are pursued, is the newlyweds' home; all the other goods are subsidiary to it.

What does this have to do with ETHICS?

If there is some end at which all persons aim, an end achievable by human action, valued for itself, and to which all other goods are subsidiary, Aristotle observes, this must be the chief good, *the highest purpose or function for man*. Let's call this "THE GOOD." To attain THE GOOD would be to realize a good life.

What is THE GOOD (for man)…or is there no such good? Aristotle finds universal agreement that *eudaimonia*—a state of well-being most commonly rendered in English as "happiness"—is such a good. However, he finds no universal agreement as to exactly what happiness is. Some identify happiness with pleasure, but beasts seem capable of experiencing pleasure and so this cannot be THE GOOD for *man*. Some identify happiness with power or honor, but this won't do either because power and honor are bestowed by others and hence ultimately depend upon the actions of others, not of oneself. Some identify happiness with virtue, but virtue is compatible with total inactivity, with being asleep, even with the greatest suffering and misfortune; virtue cannot be THE GOOD. Some identify happiness with wealth; however, wealth is not desired for its own sake but rather because it is useful for the sake of something else. Other proposals seem even weaker candidates, because they change with changing conditions. A person who is ill, for example, may identify health with happiness, but when well, that same person would offer a different candidate.

Finding only negative results with this approach, Aristotle tries a different tack. The word "good" can appear not only as a predicate or a noun but also as an adjective. Aristotle points out that this usage is tied to **function**: "good" applies when something excels at carrying out its function. Thus, for example, the function of a knife is to cut. A *good* knife cuts cleanly and easily, is nicely balanced, comfortable to hold, takes a sharp edge, and holds its edge well. That is, a good knife is a knife that performs its function well.

Importantly, and in contrast to the subjective element in the predicate and noun, as an adjective, "good" carries a measure of objectivity. If one knows what the function of a thing is, then one can judge with considerable objectivity whether that thing excels in the performance of its function or not. Now, a thing's function, if we think about it, really amounts to the good—here "good" is a noun—for which it exists. Hence, if we knew the essential distinguishing function of man, we would know objectively what it would be to fulfill that function well, and consequently we would know objectively what a good life would be.

What then is the function of man…the *essence* that is unique to the nature of man and which distinguishes man from all other species, indeed from all else? Other creatures share nutrition, growth, and perception with man. Only man, Aristotle suggests, is capable of what we might call **practical reason**.[1]

---

1. The Greek *phronesis* is usually translated as "wisdom," "practical wisdom," or "prudence," but as Aristotle's notion is of a faculty, "reason" seems more appropriate than "wisdom." "Practical reason" is often used in translations of Kant, so it is important to be aware that the two authors are talking about two distinct notions even though the same language appears in translation.

tical (as opposed to theoretical or "pure") reason comprehends ......ve thought as it pertains to voluntary decision and action. A familiar illustration comes from the story of Solomon and the two women arguing over a baby. You will remember that Solomon proposed splitting the baby in two and giving one half to each woman. By this ruse, Solomon identified the true mother who was aghast at this proposal and begged him to give the baby to the other woman instead. This is practical reason at work.

More needs to be said about exactly what practical reason is. But even without details, it seems apparent that practical reason is an essential characteristic that distinguishes man from all other beings. If so, Aristotle contends, THE GOOD (for man) must be **action in accord with practical reason**, and a good life would be one that accords with using practical reason well.

II   An Interlude Regarding Expectations

Aristotle, we noted in Chapter 1, seems to have been the first to lay out ETHICS in a systematic way; in so doing he set the stage upon which all subsequent writers on ETHICS play.

ETHICS must answer the fundamental question, "how does one live a good life?" The answer to that question will flow from a clear notion of whatever is valued above all else—THE GOOD. Accordingly, the "secret" to understanding any ethical theory is to get clear on what that theory takes as THE GOOD.

Shortly, we shall see how Aristotle cashes out his idea that THE GOOD for man is action in accord with practical reason. Before we do so, however, let us take a moment to think about ethical theories in general.

Besides identification of THE GOOD, what do we expect from every ethical theory?

Broadly speaking, a theory—any theory—comprises a set of basic principles and rules together with their logical consequences. People have developed theories concerning just about every subject imaginable. No matter what the subject, however, as "consumers" we expect our theories to satisfy certain **desiderata** (i.e., desired characteristics). The first is **clarity**. We want to understand exactly what the theory tells us, and this demands clarity. Next is **internal consistency and coherence**. If a theory is internally contradictory or incoherent, rather than answering our questions, it will simply puzzle us, raising more questions than it can answer. Third is **completeness and comprehensiveness**. The more inclusive a theory is, the greater its potential usefulness for answering our questions. Fourth, we want theories to be as **simple and concise** as possible and still meet our other desiderata. And finally, any theory that concerns "the real world" must **fit ordinary experience** wherever the theory and ordinary experience intersect.

The above desiderata apply to any theory whatsoever. Any ethical theory must also tell us what entities it applies to. Those entities, we say, have **moral standing**. Moral standing is something like legal standing; it concerns where an entity fits in a moral system and the role(s) assigned to it by the system. As providing an answer to the question of how to live a good life, ethical theories must somehow pertain to the well-being of those entities that have moral standing. Because the fundamental question is a general one, any ethical theory must also exhibit **universality**, that is, it must apply equally in relevantly similar situations to all entities with similar moral standing. And, finally, as part of its practical value, and because a good life will be a life with minimum conflict, we surely want any ethical theory to help us see how to **settle ethical disputes** or disagreements.

When we evaluate any specific ethical theory, the matter of how well it satisfies these various desiderata will always be an important consideration.

Now, back to Aristotle.

III   Golden Mean

How does one get to morality from Aristotle's notion that THE GOOD is action in accord with practical reason?

Aristotle elaborates his notion of practical reason by use of what he calls the "Golden Mean."

What is this Golden Mean? It is not a mathematical notion, like median, mode, arithmetic, or geometric mean. It is rather the *right* amount—that is, the amount that is *neither too much nor too little*— and this amount *may* differ among times and individuals. The Golden

Mean is perhaps most easily illustrated by the story of Goldilocks and the Three Bears. You will recall that for Goldilocks, one bed was too soft, another too hard, but one was just right; one chair was too big, another too small, but one was just right; and one bowl of porridge was too hot, another too cold, but one was just right. This notion of being "just right" is the notion of the Golden Mean. Presumably the hard bed would be at the Golden Mean for Papa Bear, the tiny chair at the Golden Mean for Baby Bear, and so on. The Golden Mean is the respective amount that is right for each individual. For Aristotle, the task of practical reason is to recognize the Golden Mean in all action. **Practical reason**, then, is just the ability to recognize whether something hits the Golden Mean, and if not, to recognize whether it falls on the side of excess or of deficiency.[2]

Aristotle sees in the Golden Mean a key to understanding **moral virtue**. He notices that both emotions and actions can be either deficient or excessive. Excessive fear combined with a deficit in confidence yields cowardice. A deficit in fear combined with excessive confidence yields foolhardiness. But when the right amount of fear combines with the right amount of confidence, we find courage. Cowardice and foolhardiness are vices; courage is a virtue. As a result of considering a number of vices and virtues, Aristotle contends that the case of courage is typical: each moral virtue represents a Golden Mean between vices of excess and vices of deficiency.

Moral virtue, then, is a state of character concerned with choice, lying at a mean, in this case, the mean relative to us, this being determined by a rational principle, that by which the man of practical wisdom would determine it.

It should be added that not all virtues are moral virtues. Some virtues are intellectual. How do moral and **intellectual virtues** differ?

Suppose students who know nothing about music sign up to play in the school band. Now imagine that the instructor teaches the students all about the staff, signature, note names, measures, the various kinds of notes, the "count" each indicates, and so on. After the students pass the test on this, the band instructor hands out flutes and trumpets and clarinets and trombones and so forth, and tells the students to play a song. Of course they cannot do so. To play an instrument, one

---

2. The Golden Mean need not vary among individuals. To sing middle C, a Golden Mean, one must be able to recognize both excess and deficiency in pitch and adjust one's voice accordingly.

must practice. Such practice involves trial and error *and* recognition whether the trial has hit its target or not. If on target, one tries to reproduce whatever produced that result; if off target, one tries again. In this sense, one cannot be taught to play an instrument. One can be guided, but only experimentation and practice will do the job.

Intellectual virtues, Aristotle tells us, are like the note names; they can be taught. Moral virtues, however, are like playing an instrument: that cannot be taught; it must be discovered and practiced. One becomes courageous by practicing courage—that is, by trying to find the proper balance of fear and confidence. Because the Golden Mean is only one point on an infinite continuum, hitting the Golden Mean will always be difficult.

Aristotle also advises us that, knowing we will likely miss the Golden Mean, we should always try to make our error on the side of the lesser vice.

Sidebar: Natural Law

The fall of Rome ushered in the so-called dark ages, a period in which most of the great Greek and Roman intellectual work—including most of Aristotle—was lost to Europe. During this time, however, much Greek and Roman thought was preserved in the Islamic cultures of northern Africa and the near east. Thirteenth-century interchanges between the Islamic and Christian cultures reintroduced this work to Europe, giving birth to the Medieval Renaissance and its flowering of European thought. It was then that Thomas Aquinas (c. 1225–1274) found in Aristotle a pillar for his own thought, which he synthesized with Church teachings. Aquinas argued that a rational God gave man reason and natural inclinations that enable us to discover aspects of His eternal law, or providential plan for creation, and direct ourselves accordingly. Because this law is found in our nature, it is *natural law*. Aquinas' *Ethics* grew into a highly influential tradition called **natural law theory**.[3]

---

3. In general, *natural law* includes all principles that are universal and discoverable by reason. Hence, natural law is a broadly applicable idea. It became prevalent in the seventeenth-century political philosophy that greatly influenced the founding fathers of the United States. In ETHICS, natural law theories can be found at least as far back as Epictetus (c. 50–130).

The natural law approach may be illustrated through recognition of our natural inclination to survive. In accord with this natural inclination, reason tells us to act in ways that preserve and protect life and avoid acts that destroy life. More broadly, natural law theory holds that to act rationally is to act morally, and (much like Aristotle's action in accord with practical reason) to act rationally is to act in accord with the nature, purpose, or function of things. For natural law theory, human acquisition and understanding of moral law requires only reason, not revelation.[4] Accordingly, some thinkers have felt that tying nature to God is not necessary in order to use nature and natural law as the ground of morality.

The natural law tradition identified a pair of moral principles that have been especially influential. One, the **principle of totality**, asserts that the parts of a physical entity exist to serve the good of the whole. Accordingly, any modification of a part must serve only to restore the whole to its natural and proper function. Under this principle, for example, things such as foot-binding to conform to standards of beauty and "doping" by athletes are forbidden, but surgery to repair a torn ACL would be favored.

The second principle concerns acts that have both a morally desirable and a morally undesirable outcome. The **principle of double effect** allows such acts provided four conditions are met:

1. the act itself is not evil,
2. both the good and the evil outcomes arise from the act with equally immediacy,
3. only the good outcome is intended, and
4. the good end is at least as weighty as the evil outcome.

Consider, for example, a situation where removing a threat to one's life can be achieved only by ending the life of another who poses that threat. Clearly, removing a threat to one's life is not evil in itself. The end of the threat and the death of the one threatening occur simultaneously and are unavoidably linked. Neither life is inherently more valuable than the other. Provided, then, that there is no intent to kill, only intent to end the threat, the principle of double effect allows the act of

---

4. Aquinas held that we have two sources of knowledge: reason and revelation. Reason cannot tell us everything, and God sometimes uses revelation to take us beyond reason. However—and this is a crucial point—reason and revelation must always be in harmony: true revelation and correct reason can never conflict.

self-defense. The sort of moral dilemmas that double effect addresses occur often, especially in war and in medicine, and the principle of double effect is one of very few applicable principles that ethicists of any school have been able to identify.

At their present stage of development, all existing moral theories have issues. Natural law theory is no exception. For starters, its proponents don't always agree as to what the natural inclinations of man actually are, nor do they always agree on exactly what the proper purpose or function of a thing is. This is especially true when something clearly has more than one proper use. Consider the mouth, for example. It functions for eating and drinking and speaking and even breathing. These seem to be clear, proper uses. But mouths can also be used for holding objects, for kissing, and for other things. Are these proper uses or not? (And if not, is it really morally wrong to use the mouth in such ways?) Perhaps the biggest question is whether reason alone really can tell us of any given actual use, whether it is or is not in proper accord with nature. "In proper accord with" looks remarkably like a normative notion. If it is, natural law theory must deal with issues related to jumping the fact-value gap.[5] Finally, it is very difficult to deny that men sometimes are naturally inclined to do evil, and in such cases to follow our natural inclinations would surely not produce moral action.

The genuine (dare I say, *natural*) appeal of natural law theory can only be fully realized with satisfactory responses to the issues just mentioned.

IV   "Do Ethics" and "Be Ethics"

Usually we think of ethical advice as telling us what to do, or what not to do: Tell the truth. Don't steal. Aristotle's approach is different: it tells us what to *be*, not what to *do*. For Aristotle (and, indeed, for his contemporaries) our actions are seen to flow from our character, and the job of ethical training is to develop our character in such a way that we become "all that we can be" (to steal a phrase from the U.S. Army). Aristotle's approach is often called a "virtue ethics" approach because

---

5. Discussed in Chapter 1.

it focuses on virtues, i.e., traits of good character. I prefer to call it a "be ethic" because it tells us what to be, not what to do. Most ethical theories tell us what to do; they are "do ethics."

The difference between "be ethics" and "do ethics" turns out to be less than it may at first seem. Indeed, for every "do ethic," there is a corresponding "be ethic" and vice versa. Take any proposal for THE GOOD. From that GOOD flows a "do ethic" advising us to act so as to fulfill that good. But so also flows a "be ethic" that advises us to develop our character in such a way as to promote fulfillment of that good.

In the chapters that follow, we could approach each of the central points from a "be ethics" perspective. But "do ethics" is much more familiar and so, for simplicity's sake, that's the approach we will use.

7. OR IS THERE NO SUCH THING AS THE GOOD?

Aristotle's idea that there is a highest good for man, one that is tied to the essential nature of man, opens the path to an objective foundation for ethics. Not everyone, however, agrees that THE GOOD exists.

I Non-Cognitivists, Nihilists, and Skeptics

Ethical **non-cognitivists**[1] claim that utterances regarding ethics amount to no more than commands, admonitions, and/or expressions of approval or disapproval (like grunts and cheers). As such, and contrary to appearances, declarative sentences uttered about ethics are neither true nor false. In short, there are no truths in ethics. **Nihilists** deny that there are any valid distinctions of moral value. The **skeptic** either doubts that there are moral truths, moral falsehoods, or valid distinctions of moral value, or doubts that we can know anything about purported ethical truths even if such truths exist.

None of the three would agree that THE GOOD exists.

One "cheap" argument against any claim that there are no truths about ethics is perhaps worth mentioning: that very claim is itself a purported truth. Furthermore, it is a claim about ethics. The view looks to be internally inconsistent.

Attempts to convince non-cognitivists, nihilists, or skeptics that they are mistaken usually prove most exasperating. The non-cognitivist responds to each attempt by labeling it a mere admonition; the nihilist denies the validity of any distinctions you might propose; and the skeptic claims to doubt whatever you might say.

---

1. Following tradition, we continue to use "ethical" even in cases where, given the discussion in Chapter 5, "moral" might seem a more fitting choice.

One reason not to subscribe to any of these views is that they are intellectually sterile. If there were ethical truths or valid moral distinctions or ethical knowledge, non-cognitivists, nihilists, and skeptics would never discover that there were. The nay-sayers could be right, of course, but it seems way too early to accept their negativism. The vast majority of thinkers offer reasons to believe that there are valid moral distinctions, that we probably do know some moral truths already, and that there is much promise that we will come to know more such truths. Before we reject the whole enterprise, we need at least more fully to test the possibilities.

II   Existentialists

Existentialists contend that man is unique among beings in that his essence is not predefined. For all other things, essence (purpose, function) precedes existence. For these things, the Aristotelian idea of a highest good (tied to essence or function) makes perfectly good sense. Man, however, it is claimed, is radically free and so for him, *existence precedes essence*. This principle, which unites all existentialists, teaches us that each person is born without a particular plan, purpose, or nature. What that person will be will be determined by the choices s/he makes and the actions s/he performs. No one or no thing other than oneself is responsible for one's choices or behavior: there are no excuses; each person is totally responsible for his or her thoughts and actions. Each individual's essence is under development throughout life and fully fixed only upon death. There are no "external" constraints on freedom, not even logical consistency. Thus, there is no such thing as THE GOOD for man. So say the existentialists.

The existentialist's position puts each of us in an ethically very demanding position. Since our choices and actions define who we are and since we are a part of the body of man, our choices and actions ultimately determine what mankind is. Owing to our radical freedom, there can be no pre-existing objective standards to guide us. You, as an individual, bear total responsibility for what mankind is to be, and yet you have no objective guidance. In a sense, each person is a god. Each person must create his or her own life, and each person's life is correspondingly a creation (or re-creation) of mankind. The existentialist sees the actions of each person as a "statement" or a "model" of a good life as created by that person. Others may emulate an example or not, as they choose, but the availability of example behavior or choice in no way reduces the individual's total responsibility for inventing mankind. That remains an unavoidable, heavy moral burden on every person...a burden for which there can be no guidance.

III   Subjectivists: Divine Command and Individual Relativism

Subjectivists[2] assert that ethical "truths" are "whatever"; that is, ethics is an arbitrary, individual creation. Existentialists qualify as ethical subjectivists. Strictly speaking, so do divine command theorists.

We have already discussed briefly (in Chapter 1) how religion and ethics might be related, but we did not then consider divine command theory.

In the Bible Belt, and probably elsewhere, some persons, even if they have no idea what divine command theory actually holds, will readily claim (based on the name alone) to subscribe to it. Their underlying idea is that God created the universe and everything in it, including ethical principles, that God did so by fiat, and that morality therefore originates in divine command. Of course, scientific laws originated by divine command also, and moral laws resemble scientific laws in that they are unchanging and objective. This is a perfectly reasonable (though not entirely unproblematic) idea, but it is not divine command theory as traditionally understood.

Traditionally, **divine command theory** holds that an act is moral or immoral solely *because* the divine—presumably, a god or group of

---

2. As with most terms used in philosophy, "subjectivism" is understood in slightly different ways by different persons. Here, the term is to be understood simply as the notion that the subject (person or being) is the source or point of origination of whatever is being considered.

gods—commands that it be done or not done.[3] According to this theory, morality is arbitrary in the sense that it is not a function of matters such as necessity, reason, independent principle, or some other features in the universe; rather, morality depends entirely on the possibly changing subjective preferences or chance impulses of the divine. Morality would change with each new divine command, and those commands could (in principle) be contrary to or even directly contradict previous ones. If, for example, the divine were to command that henceforth, on the eve of the summer solstice, all sixty-five-year-old persons must be slowly tortured to death, we would immediately become morally obligated to undertake such torture.

Some persons will object to this example. "God would never command that!" they say. But why not? Because, they say, torturing people to death is morally wrong (and God would never command us to do anything morally wrong).[4]

This objection misses the point entirely: according to divine command theory, the divine's specific *command* to torture, by virtue of it being *the divine*'s command, would mean that such torture ceases to be morally wrong and, instead, becomes morally obligatory. If you can't stomach that consequence, you can't subscribe to divine command theory.

Clearly, divine command theory faces all the difficulties associated with trying to find out what God says (see Chapter 1), but that's not the big problem with divine command. Once it is clear what divine

---

3. A considerable body of recent literature asserts that whatever The Divine commands is moral because of a connection to the presumed flawless nature of The Divine. It is not *that it is commanded* that makes a Divine Command moral; rather it is the inherent moral character of The Divine that does so. Early on, this approach was labeled "divine command theory." Much confusion followed (in part, perhaps, because traditional divine command theory makes no specific assumptions about the number or nature of the divine and these writers sometimes failed to note the presuppositions that were essential to what they were doing). A contemporary push to call the approach "theological voluntarism" rather than "divine command theory" hopes to avoid such confusion.

4. One might instead assert that such a command would be contrary to God's character or goodness and so could never happen. Fair enough, but this theology doesn't affect the plausibility of divine command theory itself, for the theory classically assumes nothing about the nature of the divine. Furthermore, the assertion, in referencing goodness, diverts attention from the question of what goodness (or moral character) amounts to—but that is the central question that divine command theory proposes to answer.

command theory actually comprehends, it seems quite implausible. The point is well made in Plato's *Euthyprho*. There Socrates asks simply whether an act is good because the gods love it or whether the gods love it because it is good. No argument is needed for Euthyphro (and us) to recognize the second choice as correct.

Individual ethical relativists put each person in the same shoes that divine command theorists put God in. But now, instead of morality coming from divine subjectivity, morality—if it still makes any sense to use the term "morality"—is relativized to each individual and his or her subjective whims. In short, there is no such thing as morality as we normally understand the concept.[5] Morality is without foundation and serves no function. It does not help to guide our lives or to resolve disputes. In effect, individual ethical relativism collapses into ethical nihilism, and we can reject it for the same reasons.

IV   Cultural Ethical Relativists

The cultural ethical relativist holds that what is moral or immoral is wholly relative to the culture in which one finds oneself. Anthropologists can study morality objectively in the same way that they can study any other aspect of culture objectively. But morals are not universal and objective in the same way that physical laws are universal and objective. The moral laws in each culture, according to the cultural ethical relativist, simply arise through historical accident intertwined with social and political forces.

Cultural ethical relativism turns out to be a very popular theory, widely professed by persons who haven't subjected it to critical examination.

The primary reasons to subscribe to cultural ethical relativism come from the **empirical evidence** that cultures differ and that those differences extend to mores and moral judgments. The exact same behavior regarded as highly moral in one culture might be regarded as highly immoral in another. One culture may dispose of the dead

---

5. We can't quite say that morality collapses to wants and desires—i.e., that which is good—because the relativist need not require that one's whims correlate with one's wants or desires.

by placing them on a tower and allowing the birds to eat away all the flesh; another, perhaps one that cremates its dead, will find the very thought of feeding the dead to the birds repulsive to its moral sensibilities. Such differences have been observed for centuries, but they were especially popularized and reemphasized by anthropologists such as Margaret Mead and Ruth Benedict in the early twentieth century.

The move from empirical cultural relativism, which is well established scientifically, to cultural ethical relativism depends upon a hidden premise: there exist no common normative principles that could underlie different behaviors. This premise is dubious, at best. Surely a moral principle like "thou shalt respect thy dead" underlies both the practice of cremation and of lifting the dead toward the skies on a tower to enable birds to carry the flesh towards the heavens. Different cultures show respect through different practices. How respect is shown is culturally relative, but showing respect is culturally universal.

In addition to its dubious empirical foundation, cultural ethical relativism faces a serious challenge from **cultural pluralism**. In modern society, no person belongs to just one culture. At work, at school, at church, at social gatherings, we find ourselves in different cultural surroundings. On controversial moral issues, one will likely find a whole range of norms offered by the various cultures to which one belongs. Which norm defines morality? If cultural ethical relativism were correct, the answer would be "all of them do." But then, *none* of them do…and moral choice falls entirely to the whims of the individual. In short, cultural pluralism causes cultural ethical relativism to collapse into individual ethical relativism or nihilism.

Perhaps the most telling objection to cultural ethical relativism arises with the following argument: Assume morality is, as the cultural ethical relativists say, *defined* by the current practices of a culture. That being so, any practice that differs from the current practice will be, by definition, immoral. If a practice is, by definition, immoral, there can be no sound moral argument favoring that practice. Hence, no moral argument can be used to invoke moral change within the culture. In fact, however, **moral argument** has often been used with great effect to institute **social change** and changes in cultural practices. In America, moral argument led to the end of slavery, the emancipation of women, the end of legally imposed segregation, and the promotion of equal rights for all persons. If cultural ethical relativism were correct, all of these changes would have been immoral. At present, moral argument is at work on such matters as gay rights, embryonic rights, and animal rights. Were cultural ethical relativism correct, such argument would be impossible.

V So, Is There No Such Thing as THE GOOD?

Subjectivists and relativists deny any objective ground for ethics. Ultimately, it is possible that they are correct; there is, however, little reason to think that they are. And there is at least one good reason to reject these views in favor of the objectivist view as a working hypothesis: Only the objectivist hypothesis offers us any hope that we may find solid ground. The other hypotheses stop us from looking.

Aristotle's idea that there is a highest good for man, one tied to man's essential nature, opened a path that promises an objective foundation for ethics. Before we give up on the quest, we should at least explore that path.

8. CONSEQUENTIALISM

According to an old saying, "the road to hell is paved with good intentions." This presumes that the *consequences* of our actions are what really count in moral assessment. It doesn't matter what your intentions or motives are, the outcome is everything. If you save a drowning person, you have done the morally right thing whether you did it seeking some personal reward—a moment of fame, perhaps—or because you felt some unexplained obligation to do so, or even if you simply reacted without thinking. This is, at any rate, the consequentialist take on the matter.

Any theory that evaluates the morality of an action based solely upon outcomes is called **consequentialist**. At least three competing notions of THE GOOD give rise to consequentialist ethics.

I   Ethical Egoism

How does one live a good life? Look out for number one! That's the ethical egoist's answer: when you pursue your own self-interest, you maximize your chances of attaining a good life.

One motivation for subscribing to ethical egoism has been the acceptance of psychological egoism. **Psychological egoism** is a descriptive theory alleging that persons do in fact always act in their own self-interest, at least as they perceive it to be.

Without "as they perceive it to be," psychological egoism would be pretty implausible. People often act in ways that (as any competent outsider can clearly see) are not in the actor's best interest—not even for the short run. And, of course, there are human vices, the (often habitual) actions that provide immediate pleasure or satisfaction but have adverse long-term consequences. Such actions do not promote one's true best interests. To allow for these facts, the psychological egoist must assume that persons do, upon occasion, misconceive or misunderstand what is in their best interests.

Such misconceptions create a need for ethicists to serve in, shall we say, a **therapeutic role**. If psychological egoism held true, the ethicist's appropriate job would be to help persons understand what is and is not (or would and would not be) in their best interests. Socrates and Plato seemed to have accepted psychological egoism and took exactly this tack towards ethics.

But does psychological egoism correctly describe human behavior?

Once upon a time (it is said), Abe Lincoln, riding in a carriage along a country road shortly after a heavy rain, spotted a mother pig in distress. Her piglets were unable to escape from the bottom of a roadside drainage ditch. The mud-covered banks were so slippery that the piglets tumbled to the bottom every time they tried to climb out. Lincoln ordered the carriage driver to stop, then threw his great coat on the slope, and the muddy piglets quickly scrambled up it, out of the ditch, to their mother. The carriage driver praised Lincoln for his remarkable altruism, but Lincoln would have none of it. He claimed that he had rescued the piglets purely from self-interest. Had he not done so, he said, he would have gone to bed with the images of the distressed mother and her trapped piglets in his mind and would have been unable to get a good night's sleep. As he self-interestedly desired a good night's sleep, he determined to help the piglets.

Any satisfactory descriptive theory must be **falsifiable**. That is, there must be some test by which a theoretical claim might be shown to be mistaken. The Lincoln story suggests that psychological egoism may not be falsifiable: if one wished to be dogmatic about it, one could always claim that any action whatsoever is or was done out of self-perceived self-interest, and no one could disprove this claim. Psychological egoism won't pass muster as a scientific theory.

But even without backing from a scientific theory, ethical egoism has some plausibility. **Ethical egoism** holds that one *should* act in one's self-interest. In short, THE GOOD is seen as self-interest, understood as **long-term self-interest**. Short-term or immediate self-interest too often leads to unfortunate outcomes: Overeating may satisfy my immediate interest in being nourished, but when persistently done, overeating results in obesity and cardiovascular disease. Disease is not characteristic of a good life. Self-interest, then, must be understood with a long-term perspective.

At first, the whole idea that looking out for number one will produce highly moral behavior might strike one as thoroughly implausible. Wouldn't a world full of egoists be a horrible place filled with really nasty, self-centered people? Definitely not, claim the ethical egoists. To determine what actions are in your best interests, you must consider how other persons, also looking out for themselves, will respond. If I scratch your back, you will scratch mine. If I poke you in the eye, you will poke back. Clearly, it will normally be in my long-term self-interest to treat other persons honestly and with respect. In short, ethical egoists have a direct response to the objection that their theory does not do the basic things (like resolve moral conflicts) that an ethical theory should do. They note simply that it is in their long-term self-interest to find amicable solutions to moral conflicts. Indeed, say its advocates, if you really work out the details, you will find that ethical egoism yields exactly the basic moral rules that we learn on our momma's knee.

The catch to all this is that ethical egoism tells us to follow these rules *only when it is to our long-term advantage to do so*. We should, however, break the rules whenever we can get away with it, provided only that breaking the rules would then be to our long-term advantage. This catch strikes most persons as a serious flaw in the theory. Somehow, an ethical theory that advocates breaking its own moral rules seems almost oxymoronic.

II   Radical Altruism

Ethical egoism is sometimes contrasted with a radical form of altruism—the unselfish concern for the welfare of others.[1] Instead of looking out for number one, radical altruism has us totally ignoring our own needs and looking out solely for the long-term best interests of others—that is, THE GOOD would be the long-term best interests of everyone *except* the actor.

Some of the moral teachings of Jesus seem to come very close to a radical altruism; I suspect, however, that there are very few if any genuine, radical altruists. For one thing, by totally ignoring their own needs, they would not long survive. A touch of altruism almost surely shows up in every viable ethical theory; radical altruism, however, takes altruism too far.

---

1. This contrast, like that between *richest* and *poorest*, is one of extremes and is not intended to suggest that there could be nothing in between.

III   Moral Standing

When we first examined the roots of normative predicates, we observed that morality can be understood as the expression of our strongest, most precious values...the ones we are least willing to give up or change...the ones we believe apply universally among creatures having moral standing. Such universality means that two entities may receive morally different treatment only if there is a morally relevant difference between them.

There is some confusion among ethical egoists as to whether the self-interest principle is universal or not. Should each person act in his or her own long-term self-interest, or does the egoistic principle apply solely to you or to me? Would the ideal be for me to be a radical egoist and everyone else to be a radical altruist?

This last question gives a clue to what may be the most serious objection to both ethical egoism and radical altruism: both theories make a moral distinction when there is no morally relevant difference, and thus both violate universality. For any moral theory, THE GOOD *defines* the **morally relevant dimension(s)**. All creatures who are alike in this dimension thereby have like moral standing. Thus, for example, if THE GOOD is *action in accord with practical reason*, any creature capable of acting in accord with practical reason has moral standing. Universality requires that all creatures of like moral standing in like circumstances must receive like treatment. If THE GOOD is *action in accord with long-term self-interest*, then any creature with the capacity to so act based on its judgments of its long-term self-interest must be accorded the same moral standing as any other like creature. Ultimately, ethical egoism and radical altruism fail because they assign different moral standing to those who are selected on the basis of some criterion other than the one given by THE GOOD. Thus, ethical egoism and radical altruism divide all creatures who can act in accord with long-term self-interest into two groups: me and everybody else (or you and everybody else, if you prefer). But this is a distinction without a morally relevant difference, and so it is illegitimate.

The same point can be made about **racism** and **sexism**, for example. Unless race or gender is explicitly a moral dimension flowing from THE GOOD—whatever that GOOD may be—different moral treatment based on differences in race or gender is illegitimate because it makes a moral distinction without a morally relevant difference.

IV Utilitarianism

Ethical theory remains a work in progress. As such, every theory comes in several variations, differing in detail but sharing certain common core ideas. (The common core is what makes it legitimate to apply a common name to the differing versions.) As we shall see, utilitarianism exhibits so much variation that it might better be thought of not as a single theory but rather as a family of theories bound together by agreement on the principle that *those acts are moral which produce the greatest good for the greatest number.*[2] This is called the "**principle of utility**."

To get a sense how the principle of utility works, consider this: In 1912, after having reached the South Pole (only to discover that Amundsen had beaten them by a month), Captain R. M. Scott's expedition set out on a hasty return to the safety of the coast. Unfortunately, one of Scott's explorers was injured and could travel only by being carried on a stretcher. Although knowing it would slow them dangerously, Scott decided not to abandon the man. As a result, all perished.

A utilitarian would, without hesitation, claim that Scott acted immorally. The lives of the many outweigh the life of one: Scott should have abandoned the injured man so that the rest of the expeditionary force could have survived.

Utilitarian theories tend to be ruthless in allowing absolutely no differences in treatment based upon anything other than differences that derive directly from THE GOOD. (Some regard this as utilitarianism's greatest virtue; others see it as the wellspring of its greatest flaw.) Typically, utilitarian theories are strongly universal and starkly democratic—no one counts for more or less than anyone else, but the many count for more than the one. Indeed, utilitarianism has provided a strong theoretical moral underpinning for democratic governance and for free-market economics ... and has been dominant in the formation of much public policy, most obviously policy relating to public health.

---

2. The clause, "for the greatest number," traces back at least to Francis Hutcheson in his *Inquiry into the Original of our Ideas of Beauty and Virtue* (1725, Treatise II, Section 3). It was repeated by Beccaria, Bentham, J. S. Mill, and a host of others up to and including the present day. Even so, many contemporary philosophers would not include it when stating the principle of utility.

V   Internal Problems with Utilitarianism

Utilitarians agree that the principle of utility is central to ethics, but they disagree on just about everything else. These disagreements can be grouped into four main internal problems with utilitarianism.

(1) Proponents cannot agree on what is to count as THE GOOD.[3]

The most influential utilitarian theorists have probably been Jeremy Bentham (1748–1832) and John Stuart Mill (1806–1873). They advocated what is sometimes called "hedonistic" utilitarianism. The ancient hedonists contended that the only intrinsic good is stress-free pleasure. Bentham and Mill held that the ultimate motivation for all human action is the seeking of happiness—remember Aristotle?—and they identified happiness with pleasure and the avoidance of pain; hence, THE GOOD amounts to pleasure *minus* pain. Mill supported this view with a very simple, empirical argument: The only way to know that something is visible is to recognize that it is seen. Similarly, the only way to know that something is desirable is to recognize that it is desired. As all persons desire to experience pleasure and to avoid pain, pleasure without pain is desirable!

But just as different views of THE GOOD can yield wholly different theories, different views of THE GOOD within the context of the principle of utility can yield significant differences within the utilitarian family itself. Not all utilitarians accept a hedonistic hypothesis. Some contend that happiness comes only with a plurality of goods including, for example, education, the experience of beauty, freedom, health, knowledge, peace, and power. This view is an element of so-called "pluralistic" utilitarianism. Exactly which of these goods are to be included in ethical evaluations and exactly how said goods are to be balanced out has never been settled.

Some recent utilitarians, apparently sympathetic with the pluralists (but very democratically not wanting to impose any particular set of goods on anyone), have found in the economic theory of preference rankings a happy solution. Economists have shown that it is possible to rank and compare individual preferences in a quantitative way, without any necessity for consideration of the grounds for these

---

3. One might contend that Utilitarians do in fact agree that THE GOOD is simply to *produce the greatest good for the greatest number*. However, this won't work because utilitarians don't agree about which good is to be maximized. That lack of agreement makes the proposed statement hopelessly vague.

preferences. Thus, in a sense, for these so-called "preference" utilitarians, THE GOOD is whatever is in fact most highly preferred.

Because preference can be quantitatively ranked, preference utilitarians feel they have solved the second internal problem with utilitarianism, namely,

(2) Proponents cannot agree on how to measure utility, that is, to quantify measures of goods so that the greatest good for the greatest number can be comparatively determined.

Bentham tried to produce a "calculus of pleasure" that evaluated actions as to probability of success in producing pleasure, how many would be affected, intensity of any resulting pleasure, its duration, and its fruitfulness. (Fruitfulness has to do with creating or enhancing future pleasures: if I see a movie, I might gain additional pleasure by having read the book upon which the movie is based.)

Bentham's critics, reprising the ancient hedonists' critics, charged that, pigs being as capable of pleasure as humans, utilitarianism is an ethical theory best fit for pigs. In response to this criticism, J. S. Mill tried to differentiate pleasures by quality as well as by quantity. Mill contended that "a beast's pleasures do not satisfy a human being's conceptions of happiness." Mill supported this contention with a straightforward observation:

> Few human creatures would consent to be changed into any of the lower animals for the promise of the fullest allowance of a beast's pleasures; no intelligent human being would consent to be a fool, no instructed person would be an ignoramus, no person of feeling and conscience would be selfish and base, even though they should be persuaded that the fool, the dunce, or the rascal is better satisfied with his lot than they with theirs.

In short, Mill concluded in a now-famous passage, "It is better to be a human being dissatisfied than a pig satisfied; better to be Socrates dissatisfied than a fool satisfied. And if the fool, or the pig, are of a different opinion, it is because they only know one side of the question. The other party to the comparison knows both sides" (*Utilitarianism*, Chapter 2, London, 1863).

In making this move, Mill credits some persons with expertise unavailable to others and so undermines the radical-equality characteristic of Bentham's utilitarianism. No longer can we regard each and every person as an equally important judge of utility. After all, the judge might be a fool, a dunce, or a rascal.

The move also undermines the strong moral underpinning for democratic government and replaces it with a foundation for bureaucratocracy—government by bureaucrats who presumably have special expertise in deciding what is best for the people. (Mill surely did not see this consequence and would definitely not have been pleased with it.)

There is a philosophical moral here: a seemingly minor change in a theory can have major consequences. But I have gotten ahead of myself. All that needs to be concluded here is that measuring utility is no small task and remains unsolved (except perhaps, as we said, if utility is taken to be identical with preference as the economist measures it).

We can now turn to the third internal problem with utilitarianism.

(3) Proponents cannot agree on what the maxim "greatest good for the greatest number" actually means.

To explain the problem, assume we have solved the problem of assigning total happiness points not only to each person, but (by adding) to the world itself. Now consider a population of five persons, each of whom we will identify by using the letters A–E. These persons are to inhabit one of two tiny alternative worlds, with differing amounts of happiness points in each world. The happiness distribution of both worlds is recorded in the table below. The question before us is "which of these two worlds is to be preferred according to utilitarian theory?"

Happiness Distribution in Alternative Worlds I and II

Person	World I	World II
A	3	8
B	2	1
C	2	1
D	2	1
E	2	1
	==	==
total:	11	12

Notice that World II has the greater total happiness and the greater average happiness. Notice also, however, that four persons have greater happiness in World I than they would have in World II. By contrast, only one person would have greater happiness in World II than in World I. The phrase "greater [greatest] happiness for the greater [greatest] number" is ambiguous. Depending upon whether you emphasize the "greater happiness" or the "greater number," each alternative world seems to qualify as the one with the greater happiness for the greater number.

So, does the maxim require that total good be maximized? Does it require that average good be maximized? Does it require that a greater distribution of goods goes to the greatest number (even if that means lesser total good)? Or does it require something else? Utilitarians don't agree.

This brings us to a final internal problem with utilitarianism:

(4) Proponents cannot agree whether the principle of utility governs at the level of individual acts, of rules, or of codes.

Act utilitarians say that we must evaluate each act individually, comparing it with each viable alternative in order to determine which will produce the greatest good for the greatest number. Thus, for example, if I am quite sure in one specific case that telling my friend the truth about something will cause great pain, that a well chosen lie will produce joy, and that I will not be found out, I should lie. Of course, I shouldn't always lie. Sometimes I should tell the truth. It depends on the particular case. There is no strict rule on the matter of truth-telling and lies: I should do whatever will yield the greatest good for the greatest number under the specific circumstances at hand. This is act utilitarianism.

Rule utilitarians, by contrast, see morality as inherently tied to rules. (Mill himself characterized morality as "the rules and precepts for human conduct.") Rule utilitarians are appalled at some of what act utilitarianism allows. For example, a "reality" TV series where two people fight to the death would presumably be allowed by act utilitarianism because such a series would bring great pleasure to millions of viewers, the total pleasure far exceeding the pain of the participants. Rule utilitarians see act utilitarianism as producing too many cases that come out contrary to their gut instincts, and indeed, contrary to the general rules, which, when consistently followed and in comparison to alternative rules, produce, on the whole, the greatest good for the greatest number. Such rules are, according to the rule utilitarian, the standard for judging morality. (What are these rules? They are, in general, just the commonsense ethical rules that have been worked out over the centuries and that our mothers teach us when we are children.)

Act utilitarians remain unswayed by the rule utilitarians and their concerns. Act utilitarians note that blind adherence to rules can also produce horrific outcomes. In such cases, they observe, we either over-ride the rule, basing our exception on act-utilitarian analysis, or else we modify the rule according to the details of the specific case and act-utilitarian analysis. Since act-utilitarian analysis trumps the rule, the rule itself is superfluous; only the act-utilitarian analysis matters.

Code utilitarians, also recognizing that rules have problems, are not happy with having rules selected individually, even though on utilitarian grounds. Unlike the act utilitarians, however, they suggest that the solution lies in moving "up," not "down." We must, they contend, compare entire moral codes and choose the alternative that itself, if followed uniformly, would yield the greatest good for the greatest number. Whether this can be done well enough to test, however, has yet to be seen.

Act, rule, or code? Each perspective seems to have problems that are "solved" at another level; no perspective solves all problems, and so utilitarians can't agree which perspective is best.

Sidebar: Five Cases

All of this has been pretty abstract, so let's get concrete. Here are five cases to consider. In each case, consult your intuition as to the correct moral decision. Then, work out what the various utilitarians would advise (and why). Return to these cases and do the same when we look at deontology in Chapter 9.

1. You are a switchman for a railroad. The switch you control directs the train either through a two-mile long, very narrow tunnel or across a trestle spanning a deep canyon with a river at the bottom. As no train is scheduled to go through the tunnel and some minor repair work needs to be done in the middle of the tunnel, a crew of ten has walked a mile inside the mountain and is working on repairs. You have switched the track to send trains across the trestle. Suddenly, you receive a panic call from the engineer of a train one mile away. The throttle is stuck and the train, with fifty souls on board, is barreling along at 60 mph. Two seconds after you receive this message, a barge hits the trestle's foundation and the trestle crashes to the bottom of the canyon. You

have a choice: leave the switch as it is and send the fifty on the train plunging to their deaths in the canyon or switch the train to the tunnel, saving the fifty on the train while simultaneously causing the ten workers in the tunnel to be killed by the train. Which should you do and why?

2. Five patients with the same tissue type need organ transplants to live. One needs a heart, two need kidneys, one needs lungs, and one needs a liver. A homeless person who has no living family comes into a clinic for a free checkup. This person is healthy and has the same tissue type as those who need organs. You have a choice: harvest the healthy organs from the one and save the five or send the healthy person on her way and allow the five to die. Which should you do and why?

Consider: In both cases above, one life would be sacrificed in order to save five lives. What, if any, morally relevant differences distinguish the two cases?

3. You have befriended a certified genius who is working on a cure for cancer. She is convinced that she lacks only one piece of the puzzle—and she is correct about this. One day you bring your father to meet her. As you enter her lab, she is doing an experiment. She welcomes you but says she is right in the middle of her experiment and can't stop what she is doing. She is excited, however, because she has just realized what that missing piece is. She now has the cure! As soon as she finishes the experiment, she will write it down, and then you can talk. Your dad stands just behind her to get a better view of the experiment. Suddenly, things go horribly wrong. There is an explosion, knocking the cancer doc backwards so that she bumps heads with your dad. Both lie unconscious on the floor. Fortunately, the blow is not so severe that the doctor will forget that piece that she has just figured out. Unfortunately, there are flames everywhere and they are spreading fast. You have three options: Grab the doctor and get out of there. Grab your dad and get out of there. Just get out of there. (Once you are out, the flames will not allow you to reenter and anyone left behind will be killed in the fire.) Which should you do and why?

4. You are a night watchman at a freight transfer warehouse. The warehouse is unheated and it is the middle of winter.

Leonardo da Vinci's priceless painting the *Mona Lisa* is being stored overnight pending shipment. The building has been "swept" and locked. On your 3:00 a.m. rounds, you smell smoke. You unlock the warehouse door and are horrified to see an obviously homeless person who has somehow managed to elude the sweep. He has passed out from drinking too much wine. He had built a little fire to keep warm, but once he passed out, the fire spread wildly. There are flames everywhere. You have three options: Grab the crate holding the *Mona Lisa* and get out of there. Grab the homeless fellow and get out of there. Just get out of there. (Once you are out, the flames will not allow you to reenter and the fire will destroy whatever remains.) Which should you do and why?

5. There has been a rash of technology theft on campus. Monitors, computers, DVD players, projectors, and other items are going missing. Campus security has no idea who is actually doing the thievery. However, the head cop has figured out how he can make it look like you are the thief. He presents his case to the administration officials, and they decide to build stocks in the middle of the quad. Above the stocks there is a big sign saying, "This is what happens to technology thieves at our school!" Campus security grabs you and puts you in the stocks. While you are there, the real thief wanders by and, seeing you in the stocks, decides to commit no further larceny. All technology theft stops. The head cop gets a pay raise and everyone—except you!—is happy. What does morality tell us regarding these events?

VI   External Problems with Utilitarianism

In addition to problems raised by its advocates, utilitarianism has been subjected to "outside" criticisms from those who find utilitarian theories less than promising. We have already mentioned the objection that hedonistic utilitarianism, at least, lowers morality to the level of the beasts.

The most troublesome outside objections hit act utilitarianism the hardest, and have been one motivating force behind those who advocate rule or code utilitarianism. Of the objections raised, I will mention only three:

(1) Utilitarianism undervalues rights and justice as central moral considerations. In Case 5, for example, the person in the stocks is *innocent*, but that fact does not directly affect the utilitarian calculation.

(2) Utilitarianism undervalues obligations that arise from actions (such as promising) and from relationships (such as those with family and friends). In Case 3, for example, the utilitarian would not condone giving any preference to your father if that preference arose just because he is your father.

And an objection raised notably by Kant (see Chapter 9), not only to utilitarianism but to all consequentialist theories:

(3) We can be held morally responsible *only* for what is in our control; we can predict outcomes, but we cannot control them, hence we cannot be held morally responsible for them.[4] If, for example, I let a friend stay in my house while I am on vacation, and while he is asleep a giant sink-hole swallows up the house with my friend in it, I am surely not responsible for his death.

Whether you find these objections telling or not will largely determine whether you find utilitarianism as promising as its advocates do. After we outline the steps a utilitarian follows in analyzing a situation, we will turn to utilitarianism's main competitor, deontology. As we do, compare the strengths and weaknesses of each theory, and decide for yourself which seems most promising.

VII   Putting Utilitarianism to Work

Confusion and objections notwithstanding, utilitarianism is widely subscribed to as the most promising approach towards finding an objective ethics. And confusions and objections notwithstanding, utilitarianism is quite intuitive in its application to real world cases. We may not have a way to assign numbers to overall good, but we

---

4. This external objection generates yet another internal issue: Shall we count *actual outcomes* in moral evaluation or do we count (reasonably) *expected outcomes*? A strict consequentialist would be committed to the former, but some utilitarians argue for the latter. Purists then may charge the "expectationists" with abandoning genuine utilitarianism in favor of some unusual sort of deontology (see Chapter 9).

can usually predict the likely outcome of two alternative actions sufficiently well so as to compare the resultant overall good. The act utilitarian response to the rule utilitarian suggests that utilitarian analysis is most interesting and fundamental at the act utilitarian level. The **steps of analysis** are roughly as follows:

1. Determine the relevant facts of the situation, the alternative actions (including inaction) that are possible, and identify everyone who will be in some way affected (either directly or indirectly).

2. Make the best determination you can as to what outcome each action will most likely produce.

3. Evaluate these outcomes intuitively, taking into consideration everyone affected, considering intensity, duration, immediacy (or remoteness), fruitfulness, quality, and the relative importance of each of these dimensions.

4. Choose the action that most likely produces the greatest net good for the greatest number (where net good weighs bad consequences against good).

These steps may look deceptively simple: to do them well takes serious effort and considerable practice. And even after mastery, we must be ever mindful that consequentialists can never know whether they have in fact chosen rightly or wrongly until *after* the action plays itself out. The sort of utilitarian analysis sketched above gets one no more than a "best bet."

9. DEONTOLOGY

The word "deontology" traces back to Greek words meaning "the study of duty." Deontologists totally reject the consequentialist idea that the outcome of an act determines its morality. Deontologists contend that morality turns wholly on acts and motives, and that consequences are at best peripheral to the matter. Morality, they argue (as we shall see), is fundamentally tied to **duty**. As to exactly where duty comes from and how we find out what our duties are, there is less agreement.

I Varieties

Intuitionist deontologists claim that duties—the most basic ones, at least—are self-evident or directly perceived, much as logical truths are self-evident or colors and sounds are directly perceived. The United States Declaration of Independence, which opens with an intuitionist statement regarding rights, reminds us how plausible intuitionism is. Even so, intuitionism is often challenged on the grounds that in any given situation, different persons may "perceive" different duties—duties that may conflict with or even contradict each other. Resolving such conflicts by use of intuition seems problematic, since intuition looks to be the very source of conflict. In response, intuitionists contend that the issues are in fact identical with ones regarding such things as color: persons correctly perceive color only when certain conditions are met. Disagreements about any kind of perception may arise when one or more perceivers fail to meet the relevant conditions. The real challenge is to identify the necessary conditions for accurate perception, and that is just as much a challenge for colors as for values or duties.

    Contractarian deontologists contend that duty arises with agreements—sometimes formal, sometimes merely implied—and the relationships that these agreements support. One's duties to one's child, for example, are different than one's duties to a neighbor's child. In order to live in a civilized society, every member must implicitly agree to accept certain duties (and grant the corresponding rights) to others. For contractarians, the real challenge of ethical study is to discover the conditions necessary for the legitimacy of a contract, to discover the content of actual implied contracts, and to explicate any duties that they yield.

To discover the conditions necessary for legitimacy of contracts, it should be evident, one cannot turn to contractarianism itself. One must find some independent ground. Some[1] find this ground in the mathematical theory of games.[2] Most contemporary contractarians, however, find this independent ground in formalism.

II   Formalism

Indeed, the most generally influential deontological approach is formalist. A formalist holds that *form* is the fundamental basis of classification. In ethics, this means that the form of moral claims will determine moral right and moral wrong.

In one way, the ethical formalist is like the logical formalist. Rules of inference like *modus ponens*[3] or *modus tollens* are themselves purely formal: they have no content. But when content is introduced, the form guarantees that truth will be preserved. Ethical formalism is similar: the most basic rules of ethics have no content, but when content is introduced, the rules guarantee conformity with morality. Immanuel Kant (1724–1804) has been the most influential formalist in ethics.

III   Kant's Approach

Kant developed his ethical theory in three works: *Foundations of the Metaphysics of Morals* (sometimes called *Grounding for the Metaphysics*

---

1. Notably, Canadian-American philosopher David Gauthier.

2. Game theory investigates strategies by which competing "players" can optimize outcomes in accord with their own differing interests.

3. *Modus ponens* was discussed in Chapter 3. Other formal rules of inference are discussed in Appendix B.

of Morals), *Critique of Practical Reason*, and *Metaphysics of Morals*. The first two lay out the theoretical foundations; the third examines problems of practical judgment in concrete situations.

In his *Foundations of the Metaphysics of Morals*, Kant contends that he has not discovered anything fundamentally new about ethics, but is merely clarifying what everyone already knows. He opens by praising what he calls "the good will."

All other faculties, Kant points out, are valuable for what they can accomplish. All other faculties can be used for good or evil. Only the good will can be wholly valued for itself and itself alone. Without a good will, no one would ever *deserve* happiness.

What is the will? Today, we sometimes marvel at persons whose determination and perseverance enable them to accomplish some seemingly impossible task. We say they did it "through the sheer power of their will" or "through sheer will power." That idea of will is what Kant has in mind. More precisely, Kant identifies the **will** with practical reason and explains that it is "a faculty of determining oneself to action in accordance with conception of certain laws."

The expression "determining oneself to action" somewhat awkwardly expresses the idea of autonomy (i.e., self-governance). The "certain laws," Kant tells us, are ones that can be assigned by reason alone, independent of "anthropology." Thus, in praising the good will, Kant is simply praising autonomy of the sort that can be found only among rational beings. In short, for Kant, THE GOOD is **rational autonomy**. Rational autonomy is itself intrinsically valuable, is the defining characteristic of persons, and thus is the quality that gives persons their intrinsic value.

Kant rejects the "serpent windings" of consequentialism on the grounds that one cannot be held responsible for what one cannot control. We can predict outcomes, but we cannot control them. Sometimes our most noble efforts backfire and produce only harm; sometimes our most sinister efforts backfire and benefit the target. This inability to control consequences, Kant says, means that morality cannot be tied to them. Rather, morality must be tied to what we can control, namely: motives and actions.

How, exactly, is morality tied to motives? Kant observes that acts done out of prudence or for self-gain do not seem worthy of *moral* praise. The only acts obviously deserving such praise are those that in fact go against one's own interests but are *required by duty*. To have moral worth, Kant concludes, an act must be done not only in accord with duty, but *from* duty.

Suppose an act is done from duty. It then has moral worth. But what actuates that moral worth? To understand Kant's answer, we must understand what a maxim is. A **maxim** is a (subjective) principle of action, a practical guide for volition (often expressed in a pithy form): For example, "If you want to make big money, you should go into sales," or "If you owe someone money, you must pay them back," or "Thou shalt not commit murder." For Kant, only maxims that give the motivation for our actions count as morally significant. These maxims will generally comprise some variation of the following form: "In order to achieve [specific end] in [circumstance], I will do [action]." Kantian maxims thus include purpose, but purpose differs from duty. Action, Kant contends, "derives its moral worth not from the purpose which is to be obtained by it, but from the maxim by which it is determined."

The idea is actually quite straightforward: certain principles will yield immoral actions; other principles will yield moral actions; still others will yield actions that are neither moral nor immoral. The principle of action determines the moral worth of the act it specifies.

Kant also reminds us that "duty is the necessity of acting from respect for the law." Hobbes made the same point in a quotation that we used in Chapter 5. The only difference is that Hobbes was writing of civil duty and civil law, whereas Kant addresses moral duty and moral law.

Considering these points, Kant asks what sort of law could, while totally disregarding any of its effects, determine an unqualifiedly good will. Once all effects of the law are excluded from consideration, all that remains is universal conformity to the guiding principle of law in general. Such conformity is exemplified in a single principle: *Act only in such a way that you could will the maxim of your action to be a universal law.*

Kant calls this principle **the Categorical Imperative**. An imperative, as any English teacher will tell you, is a command. "Categorical" simply means without qualification—no ifs, ands, or buts. A categorical imperative may be contrasted with a hypothetical imperative, or one that poses a condition to be satisfied before the command takes effect: "If you are in the library and must speak, speak very softly," for example. Unless the condition being-in-the-library-and-finding-it-necessary-to-speak obtains, the speak-very-softly command does not apply. A categorical imperative has no such condition to satisfy.

IV   Rational Autonomy

This very sketchy outline of Kant's introduction of the Categorical Imperative raises questions as to how one might use this principle for moral guidance. We shall turn to this matter shortly. First, however, let us more thoroughly consider the idea of rational autonomy. We can look at rational autonomy from at least two distinct perspectives. We can look at it in the abstract, and we can look at its concrete embodiment in a class of beings.

In the abstract, rational autonomy simply means governing oneself in accord with reason. To govern oneself is to create laws and act in accordance with them. To be rational, these self-created laws must conform to the dictates of reason (rather than to the dictates of emotion or prudence, for example).

A basic concept of civil law is that it shall apply universally to all who have standing as citizens. By extension, moral law must apply universally to all who have standing as moral beings. Kant's idea is really quite simple, then: All rationally autonomous beings have moral standing. Each makes self-governing laws, but each such law, if it is a *moral* law, must be such that every rationally autonomous being would willingly self-impose that same law and submit to it. It follows that an act will be moral if and only if the subjective motivating principle that governs it—that is, the maxim of the action—can rationally be generalized into an intersubjectively acceptable universal law-like statement. More particularly, if I wish to determine whether an act is moral, I must identify the maxim governing it, generalize that maxim to apply to all beings with moral status, and determine that I, as a rational person, would be willing for that generalization to be a law that I (and everyone else) must obey. Such a law will be properly understood as objective—that is, intersubjectively verifiable—because every rational autonomous being would accept it.

From the concrete perspective, we recognize that the embodiment of rational autonomy is what gives persons their great intrinsic worth: all are infinitely valuable ends in themselves. Accordingly, we can put the Categorical Imperative in a second form: *Always treat persons, including yourself, as ends in themselves, never as a means to an end only.* The "including yourself" emphasizes the universal character of the Categorical Imperative; the "only" emphasizes that others can become a means to our ends, but do so in accord with their own ends, and hence are not *used* in the pejorative sense of that word.

Since each form of the Categorical Imperative simply expresses rational autonomy as seen from a particular perspective, both forms really say the same thing and both can be expected to yield the same results when applied to real-world problems.

V   Putting Content into the Categorical Imperative

The Categorical Imperative (when viewed from either an abstract or a concrete perspective) gives us a morals-conforming pattern which itself lacks "anthropological" content. That content comes from the situations to which we apply the form as we engage in moral evaluation.

Kant observes that duties may be to ourselves or to others. He also notes that some duties are "perfect"—that is, allowing no exceptions—whereas others are "imperfect." (The meaning of "imperfect" should become clearer, shortly.) In short, there are four kinds of duties that must be considered, and we can, of course, consider each as seen from either the abstract or the concrete embodiment of the Categorical Imperative.

Let's start with the abstract perspective. Here, the Categorical Imperative tells us that we shall act only in such a way that we can will the maxim of our action to be a universal law. In short, we start with the maxim, generalize it, and then decide whether it could be willed to be law.

If it can be so generalized, any action in accord with that law is in accord with morality, that is, is morally permissible. (But remember, for Kant, action in accord with morality has moral worth only if it is *actually motivated* by the law itself.)

In applying the Categorical Imperative, it is sometimes more revealing to see what turns out to be prohibited. Consider, for example, a person who needs money. One way to get money is to borrow it. But suppose the prospective debtor knows full well that s/he will not be able to repay any loan. May s/he nevertheless borrow? To find out, we consider what maxim—what subjective motivation—could bring one to do so. I presume the maxim would be something like: "When I need money and also know that I cannot pay back any loan, I should nevertheless borrow it." Now, we must generalize this to a proposed law: Whoever needs money and knows that they cannot pay back any loan shall nevertheless borrow money.

Could a rational person will this law? Clearly not, for what would happen? Very soon, no one would lend anybody any money, and at that point it would be impossible to do as the law demands. The law would be self-contradictory in the sense that it would lead to its own destruction. Self-contradictory laws are irrational.

When a maxim leads to a self-contradictory law, action based on that maxim is forbidden and the directly opposite law presents a perfect obligation. Borrowing money only when you can pay it back (and then actually paying it back) is, therefore, a perfect obligation to others.

Here is another case: Suppose a person has some talents, but s/he is in comfortable circumstances and decides not to devote any effort to developing any of them. Is this morally acceptable? Again, we consider the motivation expressed in the form of a maxim: When I'm comfortable, I won't develop my talents. Now we generalize: No one who is in comfortable circumstances shall develop their talents. Could a rational person will such a law? This case differs notably from the one just above in that the proposed law does not in any way lead to a contradiction, so it is not irrational because it is logically flawed. Nevertheless, no rational person could will such a law.

When a maxim does not lead to its own destruction but nevertheless cannot be rationally generalized to a universal law, its direct opposite presents an imperfect obligation. Each of us has an imperfect obligation to ourselves to develop our talents. Intuitively, the obligation is imperfect, because it would be impossible to develop all our talents to the fullest. There isn't enough time. We must choose some over others.

Let's now consider a couple of cases that apply the Categorical Imperative in the form arising from the concrete embodiment of rational autonomy: *Treat persons, including yourself, always as ends in themselves and never as a means only.*

Suppose a person is depressed and contemplating suicide. Is suicide permissible? It is not. No rational person destroys that which is an end-in-itself, that which has infinite intrinsic worth. Suicide destroys the person. It is an act that uses the person as a means only (to end suffering). It is, therefore, forbidden. One has a perfect duty to oneself to live one's life. (How could you confirm that this is a perfect duty?)

Or you encounter a person who is down and out on his or her luck. Should you assist him or her? Even though down and out, the person is nevertheless a person and therefore an entity of infinite worth. And so it is indeed a duty to help others when they are in need, provided one rationally can do so. (As it would be impossible for any one person to help everyone who needs help every time help is needed, the duty to help is an imperfect one.)

VI   Objections to Kant's Formalism

There are a number of objections commonly raised against Kant's moral theory. It is claimed, for example, that the theory

(1) is abstract and difficult to apply,

(2) excludes too many acts from the moral domain,

(3) denies moral standing to small children (and animals)—but they are people too!

(4) ignores outcomes, and

(5) provides no way of choosing among incompatible acts, each of which may conform with the Categorical Imperative.

How serious are these objections?

Let us grant that the theory is abstract and difficult to apply. So what? In physics, quantum mechanics is abstract and difficult to apply. But this fact is irrelevant to what really matters, namely, whether the theory is correct.

And what about the alleged "exclusionary" character of the theory? What is excluded? No matter what act you want to consider, the Categorical Imperative will tell you whether or not that act is in accord with what is morally permissible. Thus, it does not seem to exclude anything from the moral domain that we would expect to be included. Of course, the Categorical Imperative doesn't tell us what is in the heart of the actor. Is the actor motivated by the desire to conform to moral law? Or is the motivation prudence? The real issue is perhaps whether one buys Kant's contention that whether any particular act has moral worth depends upon what is in the actor's heart. If Kant is correct, very few ordinary acts count as *moral* acts, even though fully in

accord with morality, simply because the motivation has not specifically been to fulfill a duty. Surely, however, one could choose to take a
more inclusive stance and evaluate all acts simply by whether they are
in accord with morality, leaving out the issue of motive.

To say that children or animals lack moral standing is only to say
that they are either not at all capable of governing themselves by reason or that they have a very limited capability to do so. There is nothing surprising here: we do not hold animals in any way responsible for
their actions, and we hold children responsible only to the degree that
they are rational and in self-control. This limitation does not mean
that we may mistreat or abuse children or animals, it only means that
the reasons for not doing so must come by way of philosophical argument deriving from the Categorical Imperative rather than from the
intrinsic worth of children or animals.

As for ignoring outcomes, some knowledge of outcomes clearly plays
a role in the practical reasoning one uses when analyzing a proposed universal law. (Think of what you must consider to recognize that a law
advocating borrowing when there is no ability to repay a debt is self-
destructive.) But the real issue is probably whether we accept Kant's argument regarding what he calls the "serpent windings" of consequentialism.

The fifth objection is a serious one. If deontology in general and
Kant in particular provide no way of choosing among sets of incompatible duties, each justified by the theory, deontology fails to satisfy
an important theoretical desideratum. I am inclined to say that this
objection can be largely answered by recognizing that the most widely
known of Kant's examples tend to be simplistic ones and thereby
somewhat misleading. Take the anti-suicide analysis, for example. As
Kant presents the case, suicide can never be justified. But Kant also
argued that capital punishment was the appropriate punishment for
certain crimes and indeed was the only way to respect the rational
autonomy of the person who was to be executed for having committed some heinous crime. How the maxim is cast thus turns out to be
of utmost relevance. It seems to me that it would be perfectly rational
to generalize the maxim that a person for whom natural death is very
near, for whom there is no prospect of anything more than a delay of
death, and who will suffer excruciating, unbelievable pain until freed
by death, may terminate his or her life at will. You may disagree, but
Kant held that the way to work this disagreement out is by philosophical argument. The question as to whether deontology can decide
"hard" cases remains an open one.

VII   Putting Deontology to Work

As with utilitarianism, deontology remains a work in progress with the sort of confusions and objections that that status implies. And as with utilitarianism, objections notwithstanding, deontology is widely regarded as the most promising approach towards finding an objective ethics. Indeed, as a practical matter, utilitarianism and deontology are the only two horses still in the race.

Taking all of the points raised above into consideration, we can suggest steps for a duty-based analysis, one with Kantian elements but differing from Kant in identifying the morally *permissible, obligatory,* or *forbidden* without requiring *respect for the idea of law* as *motivation.* Because deontology comes as a work in progress, we must do as we did with utilitarianism and apply the steps intuitively rather than with the strictness that a fully polished theory would allow. That being understood, here are the **steps of analysis**:

1. Determine the relevant facts of the situation, the alternative actions (including inaction) that are possible, who will be affected (either directly or indirectly) by each, and which, if any, generally recognized duty (or duties) is (or are) directly applicable.

   A. If there is no conflict among duties and no universalizable exception, these duties settle the matter.

   B. If no generally recognized duty applies, if there may be a conflict among applicable duties, or if there may be some universalizable exception to an applicable duty, continue with Step 2.

2. Determine whether the action treats persons as ends in themselves, never as a means only.

   A. If so, the action is morally permissible;[4] continue with Step 3.

   B. If not, the action is morally forbidden.

---

4. The notion *morally permissible* used here is a very weak one. It amounts to *not forbidden* and comprehends all manner of everyday trivialities (such as wearing a blue shirt, for example) that do not really involve morality at all.

    C. If the matter of respect for persons seems not to apply, the action may fall outside of the moral domain; continue with Step 3.

3. Determine whether all persons could rationally will the maxim of the action to be a universal law.

    A. If so, the action is at least morally permissible; continue with Step 4.

    B. If not, the action is either morally forbidden or falls outside the moral domain; continue with Step 4.

4. Generalize an opposing maxim, one that leads to an opposing action.

    A. If the generalized opposing maxim yields a self-destroying practice, the morally permissible action comprises a perfect duty.

    B. If the generalized opposing maxim does not yield destruction of the practice, but still could *not* itself be willed as law, the permissible action comprises an imperfect duty.

    C. If the generalized opposing maxim could also be rationally enacted (though, perhaps, not willed) as a universal law,[5] the issue is not one of morality.

As was the case with the steps of analysis for utilitarianism, to do all this well takes serious effort and considerable practice. To further complicate things, as an alternative or supplement to these steps, one may sometimes find it advantageous to analyze a problem from the flipside by taking a rights-based perspective.

---

5. If one were comfortable willing that persons always bear to the right in order to avoid head-on collisions, one should be equally comfortable with willing that persons bear to the left. There would be no irrationality in willing either instead of its alternative. Either practice would thus be morally permissible. However, one cannot rationally will *both* practices because they are mutually incompatible. Furthermore, because they are equally rational, rationality offers no preference of one over the other. Arguably, then, one cannot rationally will *either*, and so the issue is not a moral one. Of course, it is desirable to avoid head-on collisions...but how this is to be done is fundamentally a matter of prudence, not of morality.

VIII   Rights-Based Analysis

A **right** is that which is due one or upon which one has a legitimate claim. As we have already seen, rights and duties are correlative. That is, for each right there must be a corresponding duty to deliver or provide whatever is due by that right. Similarly, for every duty there will be a corresponding right. In a sense, my rights establish others' duties, and my duties are established by others' rights. (Of course, if I have a duty to myself, the corresponding right is mine as well.)

In a rather straightforward sense, then, one can think about rights as the flipside of duties, and hence an analysis from the perspective of rights would give the flipside equivalent of a direct analysis of duties.

The correlativity of rights and duties can sometimes help us analyze a particular moral case by giving us the option of looking at the problem from either or both perspectives. Suppose that Mr. Sickman volunteers to participate in a medical trial of an experimental drug intended to arrest the progress of a serious degenerative disease. After several months, it is clear that the drug not only arrests the progress of the disease in Sickman, it actually reverses it. Unfortunately, at the same time, animal studies begin to show that the drug may have dangerous side effects in a significant percentage of those who use it. On that basis (as required by law), the pharmaceutical company terminates the trial. Sickman's degeneration resumes, and he claims that the pharmaceutical company has done him wrong by withdrawing the medication. He says he has a right to health and therefore has a right to the medication.

This may sound reasonable: people do, after all, have a right to be healthy. Or do they? Let us look at this matter from a different perspective. Who is the alleged right to health a right against? That is, who has a duty to provide health? The answer is that no one does because no one can. Health is a condition, not a right. Sickman confuses his strong desire with a right.

Some persons have thought that rights are easier to figure out than duties, and consequently, that we can understand duties better by approaching moral problems from the perspective of rights. However, a comprehensive discussion of the rights theories that are actively in play today is beyond the intended scope of the present work. We'll be happy enough to master the duty perspective.

10. APPLICATIONS

I   Solving Moral Dilemmas

How does one live a good life? We have been trying to understand where the fundamental question of ethics leads us. We have rejected some proposed answers and have found merit in others. We have not yet, however, discovered an ethical theory that everybody accepts as the true foundation of morality. We have, nevertheless, identified two "families" of theories, utilitarian and deontological, that seem to show the most promise for eventually providing a universally recognized, solid foundation upon which we might justify particular claims in normative ethics.

Where, then, does our examination of ethical theory leave us in terms of **practical decision making**? If we can't decide what moral theory is the correct one, what are we to do when we are faced with an ethical dilemma? How can we decide what is morally right and what is morally wrong? Can we find common ground?

II   Prima Facie Duties

One idea that may achieve this end can be linked to a duty-based analysis that originated with Scottish philosopher **W. D. Ross** (1877–1971) in 1930.[1] Ross saw that some duties—don't murder, tell the truth, help folks out if you can at reasonable cost to you, for example—are commonly recognized as binding so long as no other generally binding duty is in conflict. (These are roughly the sorts of duties that we mentioned

---

1. In *The Right and the Good.*

in the first step of a Kantian-style deontological analysis.) Ross called such duties **prima facie duties**. (*Prima facie* is Latin for "at first view.") To figure out what duty calls for in any situation where prima facie duties conflict, we must start with philosophical argument to evaluate the relative importance of each duty in the particular situation.

Now, here is an interesting idea: Some thinkers have suggested that "produce the greatest good for the greatest number affected by an action" is a prima facie duty. If so, the notion of prima facie duties can be used to bring utilitarian considerations into a fundamentally deontological approach, giving us a sort of mixed theory. Some thinkers believe that doing so can resolve the seemingly impenetrable barrier between the two families of theories, eliminate the objections particular to each approach as it stands on its own, and give us a way to resolve any moral issue. One problem with this plan may be that it does not provide a clear way to rank obligations when they conflict with each other. Presumably, this ranking must be accomplished by use of philosophical argument, but philosophical argument based upon what?

III   Prima Facie Principles

Here is an alternative: We have pretty much narrowed the ethical field to two "teams," the deontological (including both duty-based and rights-based analysis) and the utilitarian. If both teams give us the same moral advice in a particular case, we can be pretty sure that that advice is morally warranted, even if we aren't exactly sure what the true nature of that warrant may be. In other words, if we analyze a particular moral problem from both a deontological and a utilitarian perspective, and if each theory yields the same answer, that answer will be the common-ground answer we need.

Of course, going all the way back to THE GOOD or any other fundamental theoretical foundation will be a lot of work. Would it be possible to simplify the job by extracting some general principles that flow from *both* utilitarianism and deontology? Taking a hint from Ross, we might call these **prima facie principles**. These would be principles that we could regularly turn to as our primary instrument for moral analysis.

As it happens, there seem to be four such basic moral principles that nearly all moral theories—not just the deontological and utilitarian—support. These prima facie principles focus upon autonomy, nonmaleficence, beneficence, and justice.[2]

IV   Autonomy

The moral principle of **autonomy** tells us that, unless there is an overriding moral reason to do otherwise, we must respect the informed choices of rational, self-governing beings.

What, in this case, does "respect" mean? First, it means that we must not take steps that hinder or prevent a rational, informed agent from carrying out his or her will (unless, of course, carrying out that will would violate autonomy or bring injustice or harm to another). It also means that in our interactions with others we must not conceal factual information that would be relevant and necessary to them to make an informed decision. And finally, it means that we may choose to help others carry out their will. Indeed, the principle of beneficence—see below—encourages us to do so, especially when there would be little or no cost to ourselves.

Deontologists would support the principle of autonomy as an obvious instance of the second form of Kant's Categorical Imperative. Utilitarians would support it on the grounds that one gains utility from doing what one wills to do and suffers when that will is frustrated.

The principle of autonomy has important implications for interactions where one party has expertise or knowledge that the other party does not have and could not easily get. In medicine, for example, the principle demands that patients be given unbiased information about the positive and negative effects of any proposed tests or treatments. In sales and marketing, autonomy requires that products or services, particularly technically advanced products or services, must not be misrepresented to potential customers as to either costs or benefits.

The principle of autonomy also has implications for public policy and civil law. John Stuart Mill captured the idea nicely through the

---

2. Some would add veracity (truth telling), fidelity (promise keeping), and perhaps other duties to this list. Doing so sharpens the focus on these additional principles. I include only four because I am inclined to think that most (if not all) proposed additions are inherent in those four.

"principle of harm" defended in his treatise, *On Liberty* (1859). Mill asserted that "the only purpose for which power can rightfully be exercised over any member of civilized community, against his will, is to prevent harm to others. His own good, either physical or moral, is not a sufficient warrant...Over himself, over his own body and mind, the individual is sovereign."

A society—especially a democratic society—must assume that its members make decisions in an informed and rational way. That being the case, society has no right to criminalize or even prohibit any behavior that directly harms no one other than, possibly, the actor. To do so would be to disrespect that actor's autonomy. Having no moral right to restrain "private"—that is, purely personal—behavior, the society is morally prohibited from doing so. This moral restriction on civil lawmaking rises directly from the principle of autonomy as limited by the principle of nonmaleficence.

V Nonmaleficence

The moral principle of **nonmaleficence** (non-ma-LEF-i-cence) tells us that, unless there is some overriding reason to do otherwise, one's actions should not inflict evil or harm. Deontologists (who would unquestioningly accept this as a universal law) and utilitarians (who see all evil or harm as contrary to achieving the greatest good) would obviously support this principle.

To practice nonmaleficence, one must avoid the infliction of harm. The challenge therein (and the challenge in any related moral argument) is to determine what would or would not inflict harm...or, perhaps more fundamentally, what would or would not be a harm. This task would be much easier if we had a clear way to explain just what *harm* is. Unfortunately, we do not.

Consider, for example, the fundamental principle of nonmaleficence directly expressed in the physician's oath, "First, I will do no harm." Suppose a surgeon makes an incision prior to excising an internal cancerous growth. Does that incision do harm? Perhaps it does, but the harm is permissible because of the overriding benefit (removal of a cancer) to follow. On the other hand, even though tissue is damaged, perhaps no harm is done. "Harm" is evidently a normative (rather than a descriptive) term. As such, harm may be highly context dependent, and determining whether harm occurs may require significant normative argument.

It may also be (as the intuitionists claim) that "harm" is, like "red," a primitive term—a term that can be understood but not defined. It seems more likely, however, that "harm" is simply a very hard notion to get a precise handle on. Harm is in some sense the opposite of benefit, but exactly how this might clarify our understanding is elusive. Harm seems somehow linked with damage, but whereas damage can be purely cosmetic, harm cannot. Harm seems also somehow linked with the interests of beings having moral standing: we cannot harm a stone; we can harm a person. This suggests that we must be very careful not to identify any physical change with a harm: a physical change may result in a harm, but the change isn't itself the harm (or the benefit, for that matter).

The concept of *harm* and the principle of nonmaleficence are central to a number of "hot" issues: abortion, euthanasia, capital punishment, and experimental medicine, to name a few.

Nonmaleficence provides a moral foundation for the admonition "Thou shalt not kill." This admonition as stated, as with the traditional formulation of the Golden Rule, must be understood as incomplete. "Kill" is a purely descriptive term. In the food chain, humans are absolute consumers; we cannot live without killing. Normative import comes only when killing incorporates harm, but not all killing harms. This is understood when we "correct" the admonition by appending some phrase like "innocent persons" to it.

"What would be the harm?" "What would make it a harm?" These are the basic questions we must answer as we turn to the principle of nonmaleficence for moral guidance.

VI   Beneficence

The moral principle of **beneficence** tells us that, unless there is some overriding reason to do otherwise, one's actions should serve to provide benefit, whether by promoting good, preventing harm, or removing evil. Any action that supports autonomy would count as a benefit. Thus, for example, autonomy requires that one not conceal factual information that would be relevant and necessary to another person making an informed decision. Beneficence adds a further, positive duty to be sure that all of the information actually necessary to make a rational, well-informed decision be made available. It is, for example, not enough merely to answer a customer's questions honestly; beneficence calls upon us to also answer the questions that the customer does *not* ask…but should!

The principle of beneficence clearly promotes the utilitarian idea of the greatest good for the greatest number and also coincides nicely with one of Kant's examples of an imperfect duty. It is surely consistent with the Golden Rule of the Christian Gospels: Do unto others as you would have them do unto you.

Beneficence carries the risk that it may be—and perhaps often is—overdone. When someone claims to have done something for someone else's "own good," chances are that the someone else did not wish whatever was done to have been done, and that what was done constituted a violation of autonomy. An alternative form of the Golden Rule, "Do not do unto others that which would be hurtful to you," was perhaps formulated in the negative by an author who recognized the dangers of overextended beneficence.

But even this negative formulation falls short of solving the problem. In both forms, the Golden Rule presupposes that what you and I would desire in a given situation will always be the same. In fact, however, you might find the way that I would wish to be treated were I in your position to be strongly contrary to your wishes or even hurtful to you. This suggests that the Golden Rule should explicitly incorporate **empathy**. Empathy obtains when one has the same thoughts and feelings that another has.

Perhaps, then, as with so many pithy traditional sayings, we must regard the Golden Rule as incompletely stated. A richer formulation would be, "Do unto others as you would have them do unto you *if you were them in their situation.*" This expresses the essence of beneficence.

VII   Justice

The moral principle of **justice** tells us that, unless there is some overriding reason to do otherwise, one's actions should serve to bring what is due to whom it is due. This principle closely relates to Kant's idea that duty is tied to moral law and to our earlier observation that the notion of justice arises as a correlative concept coincident with the appearance of the idea of law. Utilitarians would agree that everyone getting what they are due will likely produce the greatest good for the greatest number.

Justice as a political idea (i.e., equal treatment of citizens under the law) naturally extends to a moral ideal: Treat similar kinds in similar situations similarly, without prejudice or bias.

The first practical problem of justice is to determine whether two entities are of similar kinds. Here, **kind** is a moral category comprising all entities with the same moral standing. Whether a particular being is of a particular kind must be determined by what objective qualities that being has and what objective qualities characterize that kind. For moral categories, it is essential that only qualities having basic moral significance—qualities such as the ability to suffer, to reason, and to act upon self-chosen principles—serve to define the category.

Mankind has not always lived up to this standard: Primitive man seems to have granted moral standing only to members of his tribe; for centuries, slaves and women were widely regarded as property with no greater moral standing than other property.

Classifications based on qualities not tied to moral foundations— classifications based on accidents of birth, of gender, of race, of color, or of creed—fundamentally violate the moral principle of justice. Moral growth of and within a society occurs as that society sheds the morally extraneous from those criteria it uses to separate moral kinds.

The other practical problem of justice is to determine the limits of similarity. If we are to treat similar kinds in similar situations similarly, without prejudice or bias, we must determine when two different situations are similar enough to call for similar treatment. Here, judgment is called for. That judgment must be guided by the recognition that equal treatment is not necessarily identical treatment, but rather is treatment based on equal consideration of the interests of all parties involved.

VIII   Judgment

Prima facie principles are to be followed except when in conflict with an equal or stronger principle. Clearly, the principles of autonomy, beneficence, nonmaleficence, and justice may in certain circumstances come into conflict. When this happens, we must *judge* what balance best resolves or minimizes the conflict. To a degree, we may be aided by recognizing a prima facie hierarchy. Autonomy surely stands above the others. If an act of beneficence would cause harm, the principle of nonmaleficence holds sway. Justice may be tempered by beneficence, provided, of course, the beneficence is not so excessive as to cause harm. When the combined principles fail to narrow our choices sufficiently, allowing for too many options, one may wish to turn to the principle of utility—a possible fifth prima facie moral principle—for the final refinement.

Judgment may be wise or foolish. In morality, wise judgments come with experience and practice, using calm deliberative reasoning supported by clear concepts, sound moral principles, and open consideration of all relevant facts.

I hope that you will find this hornbook for ethics of lasting value as you face life and seek to make wise moral judgments.

Appendix A. Critical Thinking

I Claims

A **claim** is a statement (declarative sentence) that is asserted as true.
- A claim is *true* or *false* according to whether it in fact corresponds to reality or not.
- A *descriptive* claim presents a picture, account, or report. [My life is finite.]
- A *normative* claim gives a rank, value, or judgment. [My life is wonderful.]
- The degree to which a claim is normative or descriptive often falls on a continuum and depends less on form than on use. [To claim that a particular color sample is "mauve" is primarily to describe, but a certain element of judgment is also involved.]
- A *factual* claim alleges that something is actually the case. "Factual" is often used as a synonym for "descriptive," but speaking strictly, factual claims can be either primarily descriptive [The moon is cube-shaped.] or primarily normative [Murder is immoral.].
- An *objective* claim is basically a *subjective* claim that is commonly agreed to.
- The proper contrasting term for "opinion" is "knowledge" (not "fact").
- A *concrete* claim or example is one with a low degree of abstraction.
- An *analytic* claim is one in which the subject contains the predicate.
- A *synthetic* claim is one in which the predicate adds to the subject.

- An *a priori* claim is one for which evidence is irrelevant to evaluating its truth.
- An *a posteriori* claim is one for which evidence is necessary to evaluate its truth.
- Synthetic *a posteriori* claims concern **matters of fact** whereas analytic *a priori* claims concern **relations of ideas**.

II Argument

An **argument** (as understood in philosophy) is a *series of statements*: some statements are **premises**; the rest are **conclusions** that are **inferred** from previous statements. (Argument is our best tool for analysis and evaluation of claims and concepts.)

Success in argumentation requires that one find *common ground* in both the premises and the principles of reasoning (inferences) used.

A **reason** is a factual statement (i.e., descriptive claim), definition (i.e., explication of concept), or statement of principle *that serves as an essential premise in an argument.*

A **position** is a statement that resembles a mere opinion but differs from opinion in that it is backed up by reasons and argument(s).

An argument can be evaluated as to whether it
- has an interesting conclusion (otherwise: nobody cares!)
- has solid premises (otherwise: garbage in, garbage out.)
- is well reasoned—the premises actually support the conclusion (otherwise: so what?)

Solid premises command acceptance by any (thoughtful) person who encounters them:
- Factual premises should be verifiable by objective, empirical means.
- Definitional premises should be absolutely clear and transparent, and (when appropriate) they should capture the common meaning of the term defined.
- Premises that state principles should be such that to ask "why?" of them would seem somehow inappropriate…or even impertinent.

An **inference** is the move from one or more statements to a statement (a *conclusion*) that presumably *follows from* the original statement(s).

- The measure of an inference is how well it *preserves truth*.
- **Deductive** inferences, when successful (valid), totally preserve truth: it *is not possible* simultaneously for the premises to be true and the conclusion false. Deductive validity is the "gold standard" of inferences and is a function of *form* alone.

  Examples [*P* and *Q* represent statements; '*NOT*' is short for "It is not the case that"]:

  1. If *P*, then *Q*. *P*. Therefore, *Q*. [*Modus ponens*]
  2. If *P*, then *Q*. *NOT Q*. Therefore, *NOT P*. [*Modus tollens*]
  3. All *A*s have property *p*. Therefore, this particular *A* has property *p*. [*Universal instantiation*]
  4. This particular *A* has property *p*. Therefore, something has property *p*. [*Existential generalization*]

  [NOTE: An inference may be valid even if a premise is false. Valid inferences drawn from premises that are in fact true are said to be *sound*.]

- **Inductive** inferences, even when successful (*cogent*), do not guarantee preservation of truth: it *is possible* (though perhaps unlikely) simultaneously for the premises to be true and the conclusion false. A conclusion drawn through cogent inductive inference is (presumed to be highly) *probable* but *might be false* even if all the premises are true.

  Common inductive inferences are:

  1. Abduction: *P*. *Q* is the best explanation for *P*. Therefore, *Q*. [Sherlock Holmes (mistakenly) called this "deduction."]
  2. Analogy: *A* closely resembles *B* [i.e., they both have properties *p, q, r, s, . . .*]. *A* has property *z*. Therefore *B* has property *z*.
  3. Generalization: A_1 has property *p*. A_2 has property *p*. A_3 has property *p*, . . ., A_n has property *p*.
     a. Therefore A_{n+1} will have property *p*. [or]
     b. Therefore, all *A*s have property *p*.

4. Abstraction: "pulling out" a "relevant" distinguishing
   feature [a "universal"] from a class of individuals.
   Abstraction may be thought of as a special type of
   generalization.

Disputes arise whenever there is disagreement or misunderstanding
about either
- Concepts
- Facts
- Principles, or
- Reasoning

Things can go wrong, therefore, whenever:
- People operate with muddled concepts—concepts are
  logically prior to facts: *FIRST: get your concepts straight!*
- People get their facts wrong—urban legends and so-called
  common knowledge may be widely accepted as fact, but
  shouldn't be. Check out your facts by turning to reputable, peer
  reviewed studies or to experiences that anyone can duplicate.
- People make specific claims without recognizing that the
  claim is an instance of a principle that may be goofy or that
  they would reject for some other reason.
- People reason badly.

Here are some other common errors in thinking:
- Use of abstract terminology for which the user lacks
  sufficient concrete experience to understand what the
  terminology actually means.
- Failure to see a problem in a sufficiently large context to
  make sense of its true significance.
- Generally confused or muddled reasoning.

Here are some common muddles:
- Drawing straightforwardly invalid inferences—what possible
  excuse could there be for such foolishness?
- *Equivocation*—switching meanings in midstream. This can
  occur either when one word switches meanings or when one
  homophone replaces another.
- *Question begging*—to avoid an issue entirely (often by asking
  a rhetorical question) or to offer as a reason for a particular

conclusion a disguised version of that conclusion itself
(sometimes called "circular thinking").
- Diversions—either replacing one matter by another
(as when the anti-evolutionist mocks the real issues by
asking if anyone really believes that the chimpanzee is his
grandfather), or replacing a strong view with a weak one and
attacking the latter (a "straw man").
- Unwarranted presuppositions—"Do you *still* beat your wife?"

III   Counter Example

A **counter example** is a specific case that demonstrates the falsehood
of a general claim or the invalidity of an argument.
- To show the *falsehood* of a general claim, give a clearly false
instance of the claim. [Example claim: No one can make a
difference in this world. Counter examples: Adolph Hitler,
Jesus of Nazareth . . .] (A powerful way to criticize a premise
is to show that it is false by giving a counter example.)
- To show *invalidity*, produce a specific scenario such that
in an exactly parallel argument—that is, one that has the
same form—the premise or premises are clearly true and the
conclusion is clearly false. This can be done either formally
or informally. (A powerful way to criticize an argument is to
show that it is invalid by giving a counter example.)
- Invalid arguments that seem somewhat plausible often
require an additional premise to make them valid. Frequently,
these suppressed premises are easily seen as false once they
are made explicit.

IV   Argument Analysis

- Determine if an essential premise is missing; if so, add the
premise. (Also, delete any inessential premises.)
- Determine whether the premises are true. (Are there any
counter examples? Reject arguments with any false premises.)

- Be alert to premises that simply state the conclusion using different words (begging the question).
- Be alert to emotion-laden, rhetorical terminology...it can cloud reason.
- Be alert to any inference from the descriptive to the normative. Such a jump **must have** a linking premise. (Failure here is called "jumping the fact-value gap.")
- Be alert to ambiguities...a midstream switch in meaning (equivocation) is a too common mistake.
- Any switch from one category (e.g., ideas, brains) to another (e.g., existence, minds) is suspect.

Specifically regarding deduction:
- Determine whether the inferences are valid. (Is there a counter example? Reject arguments that depend upon any invalid inferences.)
- All valid deductions presumably trace back to the *law of (non)contradiction* (no thing can both be and not be *p*) and/or the *law of the excluded middle* (each thing either is or is not *p*).

Specifically regarding induction:
- Abductive arguments fail if there is a better explanation.
- Analogical arguments fail if the analogs are not close enough or if one of the analogs is a part of the other.
- Generalizations fail if the sample size is too small, biased, or otherwise unrepresentative.
- Abstractions fail if the sample size is too small, biased, otherwise unrepresentative, or if the resulting concept leads to paradoxes or antinomies.

Appendix B. Deductive Forms

As noted in Chapter 3, an *inference* is the move to a statement that presumably follows from one or more prior statements (called *premises*). We are particularly interested in *valid* inferences, that is, those wherein the conclusion really does follow deductively from the premises. By "really does follow deductively from" we mean that it would be impossible simultaneously for the premises to be true and the conclusion false; true premises "guarantee" that the conclusion will be true also.

I   Sentential Connectives

As it turns out, the validity of a number of inferences turns on just a few words.

Consider the following sentences:

> B.1 Either animals feel pain or it is not the case that animals feel pain.
> B.2 It is not the case both that animals feel pain and that it is not the case that animals feel pain.

These two sentences are awkwardly worded. Normally, we would say something like "Either animals feel pain or they don't," and "It is not the case that animals both do and do not feel pain." Whether in the awkward form or the stylistic variant, these sentences are obviously true. A bit of thought will show that the keys to their truth lie in the expressions "it is not the case that...," "either...or ___," and "both...and ___" (or their stylistic variants). These expressions, along with "if...then ___," and "... if, and only if ___" (and a number of stylistic variants), connect declarative sentences to make new declarative sentences; hence, they are called **sentential connectives**.

Sentential connectives provide logical structure.

To help focus on that structure, it is advantageous to abbreviate each distinct declarative simple sentence by a unique letter of the alphabet, producing a **scheme of abbreviations**. In the example above, there is only one distinct simple declarative sentence, so all we need is one abbreviation. Suppose we abbreviate the simple sentence "Animals feel pain" by the capital letter 'P'. Now, we uniformly replace the sentence with that letter. If, in addition, we substitute the simple 'NOT' for the awkward "it is not the case that," we end up with schematic sentences that nicely display the essential logical form:

> B.1′ Either P or NOT P [law of the excluded middle].
> B.2′ NOT both P and NOT P [law of contradiction].

As the bracketed additions suggest, these two forms have been given names. The first is called the "law of the excluded middle," the second is called the "law of contradiction." Some think that these two laws provide the most basic principles of reasoning. In any case, it should be clear that no matter what declarative sentence you choose to substitute for the 'P's in B.1′ or in B.2′, the sentence you end up with will always be true.

II   Valid Inferences

Recall now that a valid inference is one that will never allow us to move from truth(s) to falsehood(s). Using a horizontal line to mark the inference, some patterns that are known to preserve truth (and the names of these patterns) are listed below. In every case, it would be impossible for the premises to be true and the conclusion simultaneously false. To convince yourself of this, it might help to specify a scheme of abbreviations and use it to flesh out each of the patterns. It shouldn't take much time to persuade yourself that no matter what specific sentences the letters 'P', 'Q', and 'R' abbreviate, you will never find a combination where the sentences above the lines are true while the one below it is false.

1. Reiteration:

> P
> ─────────── [reiteration]
> P

2. Simplification:

P and Q
_____ [simplification]
P

3. Adjunction:

P
Q
_____ [adjunction]
P and Q

4. Dilution:

P
_____ [dilution]
P or Q

5. *Modus Ponens*:

If P, then Q
P
_____ [*modus ponens*]
Q

6. *Modus Tollens*:

If P, then Q
NOT Q
_____ [*modus tollens*]
NOT P

7. *Modus Tollendo Ponens* (also called "disjunctive syllogism"):

Either P or Q
NOT P
_____ [*modus tollendo ponens*]
Q

8. Separation of cases:

> Either P or Q
> If P, then R
> If Q , then R
> _____ [separation of cases]
> R

Of these eight, the first three are so obvious that people use them without even realizing that they are drawing inferences. Dilution isn't normally all that useful. But *modus ponens, modus tollens, modus tollendo ponens*, and separation of cases underlie an exceptional fraction of interesting arguments. We used separation of cases, for instance, to establish the prima facie principles emphasized in Chapter 10. It also shows up in "damned if you do, damned if you don't" arguments. As another example, consider the following scheme of abbreviations:

> P: Utilitarianism is the correct moral theory.
> Q: Deontology is the correct moral theory.
> R: We should help our neighbors when we can do so at little or no cost to ourselves.

Interpreting 'P', 'Q', and 'R' in separation of cases using this scheme, we obtain the following variation of the argument used to establish the prima facie principle of beneficence discussed in Chapter 10:

> B.3 Either utilitarianism or deontology is the correct moral theory.
> B.4 If utilitarianism is the correct moral theory, we should help our neighbors when we can do so at little or no cost to ourselves.
> B.5 If deontology is the correct moral theory, we should help our neighbors when we can do so at little or no cost to ourselves. Therefore, (by separation of cases)
> B.6 We should help our neighbors when we can do so at little or no cost to ourselves.

III   Invalid Inferences

In Chapter 3 we discussed two invalid inferences that are so egregious and so common that they are worth restating. These forms *do not* preserve truth. Do not make the mistake of being misled by either!

9. Fallacy of affirming the consequent:

If P, then Q
Q
_____ [INVALID]
P

10. Fallacy of denying the antecedent:

If P, then Q
NOT P
_____ [INVALID]
NOT Q

IV   Quantifiers

In the examples above, sentential connectives provide the logical structure. Logical structure also comes with the so-called "quantifiers," "each" (stylistic variants: "every," "all") and "some" (stylistic variants: "there exists," "there is/are").

The validity of the inferences from

B.7 Each horse is a mammal.

and

B.8 This is a horse.

to

B.9 This is a mammal.

and from

B.10 Each horse is a mammal.

to

B.11 Each horse's head is a mammal's head.

depend upon the logical structure provided by "each."

Overall, quantifier logic is somewhat more challenging than sentential logic. That said, two inference rules for quantifier logic are pretty straightforward: **Universal instantiation** allows us to assert any specific instance of a universal claim. Thus, for example, we could move from "All things are material" to "This specific thing is material." **Existential generalization** allows us to move from the claim that a specific thing has a certain property to the claim that *something* has that property: "This cow is bovine; therefore *something* is bovine." Rules that allow us to make universal generalizations and existential instantiations are also known, but these rules are complicated by very strict limitations, and laying them out in detail goes far beyond what is possible in a brief appendix such as this.

So for now, the important things to remember are that, just as with sentential connectives, quantifiers give logical form, one can judge the validity of arguments based on that form alone, and one can demonstrate invalidity of a given argument by creating an argument that is parallel in form but has clearly true premises and a clearly false conclusion.

Remember also that an argument can be valid even if the premises happen to be false. Validity keeps us from going from truth to falsehood; it does not guarantee that we start with truth. When evaluating arguments, we must evaluate the truth of the premises independently of validity. If the premises are true, however, validity assures us that the conclusion will also be true.

Appendix C. Suggestions
For Further Reading

There are almost unlimited paths of exploration in the ethical forest. One can explore systematically if one chooses, but I would encourage wandering along whatever path looks appealing, following your muse, and discovering where it leads. There is no better place to start than with a specific concept or a particular philosopher's name and a visit to the *Standford Encyclopedia of Philosophy* (http://plato.stanford.edu/) or the *Internet Encyclopedia of Philosophy* (http://www.iep.utm.edu/). Here a word search will take you to excellent, authoritative articles that will invite you along other trails to explore and provide extensive bibliographies as signposts to guide you. Often you will be led to articles in scholarly journals; these can very often be found at JSTOR (http://www.jstor.org/), a subscription database that you can access through almost all academic (and many public) libraries.

Another great starting place would be an anthology containing a selection of classical and modern readings. These grab the best statements of great minds and will give you a sense of how ethics has developed over time via a 2,500-years-long transgenerational dialogue. An excellent, reasonably priced contemporary example of this genre is Louis P. Pojman and Peter Tramel's *Moral Philosophy: A Reader* (Hackett). Other highly regarded (but much more expensive) anthologies include Peter Singer's *Companion to Ethics* (Blackwell), Russ Shafer-Landau's *The Ethical Life* (Oxford), James Rachels' *The Right Thing To Do* (McGraw-Hill), and Mark Timmons' *Conduct and Character* (Cengage), among others. Timmons' *Disputed Moral Issues* (Oxford) and David Boonin and Graham Oddie's *What's Wrong?* (Oxford) are examples of collections that focus on contemporary issues (e.g., abortion and animal rights). You generally need not worry about getting the very latest edition of any ethics anthology. Older editions found at your local used bookstore or online at AddAll.com and Amazon.com are fine. The classic writings haven't changed, and even anthologies published as far back as the 1950s will give you plenty to think about…and pique your interest in new paths to explore.

For those so inclined, it can be great fun to jump back to the birth of philosophical ethics by reading Plato's classic works that focus on ethical problems: *The Republic, Protagoras,* and *Gorgias.* These introduce almost every basic problem and consider possible solutions. Other classic, seminal works are also fun to study. The most ancient "textbook" is Aristotle's *Nicomachean Ethics.* The classic presentation of utilitarianism is Jeremy Bentham's *An Introduction to the Principles of Morals and Legislation* and a powerful defense is given in John Stuart Mill's *Utilitarianism.* Kant's theory is laid out in his *Foundations of the Metaphysics of Morals* (sometimes called *Grounding for the Metaphysics of Morals*), *Critique of Practial Reason,* and *Metaphysics of Morals.* (The first two lay out the theoretical foundations; the third examines problems of practical judgment in concrete situations. Be forewarned, Kant is notoriously difficult to read and, consequently, widely misunderstood). One of the most influential works of the twentieth century is G. E. Moore's *Principia Ethica.*

All of these classics are available in very modestly priced editions either from Dover Publications (http://doverpublications.ecomm-search.com/search/Category-Philosophy_and_Religion--keywords-ethics) or from Hackett Publishing (http://www.hackettpublishing.com/philosophy/moral-philosophy). Hackett's volumes usually have more contemporary translations than Dover's. Many more great books can be found in the lists of these two publishing houses, including works by Maimonides, Schopenhauer, Nietzsche, and Hegel, for example, that offer perspectives we have not been able to cover in this volume.

If you are intrigued by our discussions of language and critical thinking, you will probably enjoy S. I. Hayakawa's *Language in Thought and Action* and Peter Farb's *Word Play: What Happens When People Talk.* Both were last published in the 1990s but are still available through online sources. Aristotle's *Rhetoric* and Alfred Jules Ayer's *Language, Truth, and Logic* are also fun. S. Morris Engel's *With Good Reason: An Introduction to Informal Fallacies* (Bedford/St. Martins) gives a nice look at common blunders. Theodore Schick, Jr., and Lewis Vaughn's *How To Think About Weird Things* (McGraw-Hill) looks more deeply at the general problem of what we can know and how we can know it.

Bioethics and business ethics are perhaps the hottest areas in ethics today, and books covering the latest developments are constantly being issued. Two outstanding, compact introductions to ethical problems in medicine and biological research are Gregory C. Pence's *The Elements of Bioethics* (McGraw-Hill) and Robert M. Veatch's *The Basics of Bioethics* (Prentice Hall). Joseph DesJardins presents comprehensive yet compact discussions of ethical issues in business in *An Introduction to Business Ethics* (McGraw-Hill).

I have barely scratched the surface here, but I hope the scratch is enough to give you a good start. As you continue your study of ethics, let your heart be your guide. Read what interests you, and do not be afraid to follow leads wherever they may go.

Index